D1880952

THE

MAHARAJA OF CASHMERE

THE

MAHARAJA OF CASHMERE

A VINDICATION

AND

AN APPEAL

JOGENDRA CHANDRA BOSE, M. A., B.L.

GYAN

Published by

GYAN

Gyan Publishing House
5, Ansari Road
Daryaganj, New Delhi-110002
Phone: 011-47034999, 9811692060
E-mail: books@gyanbooks.com

Distribution Network
gyanbooks.com
India, USA, Canada, UK, Australia, France

ISBN : 978-81-212-9214-6 (PB)
First Published, 1893

2nd Impression 2023

Printed at: Gyan Press, Delhi.

THE MAHARAJA OF CASHMERE
Author: JOGENDRA CHANDRA BOSE

THE MAHARAJA OF CASHMERE

A VINDICATION

AND

AN APPEAL

BY

JOGENDRA CHANDRA BOSE, M.A., B.L.,
of the Punjab Chief Court Bar.

CALCUTTA:
1893.

CONTENTS.

Preface.—page xi.

Introduction.—page 1.

Object of the book—The Viceroy's visit to Cashmere—Position of the Maharaja bettered—The reparation done to him not enough—Position of the Paramount Power in India in connection with the Native States—Importance and utility of the Native States—Sympathy felt for them throughout the country—They afford careers to the people of the country—They are remnants of former political independence and landmarks of an ancient civilization—They patronise learned men and protect the indigenous arts, industries and manufactures—They are centres of self-government—Lord Lansdowne on Native States and self-government—Native States are pillars of the empire—Annexation policy of Lord Dalhousie—The services of the Native States during the Mutiny—Lord

Canning—Other eminent statesmen on the value and usefulness of the Native States—The Royal Proclamation of 1858—The rights and privileges of the Native States finally secured to them—Duty of the Paramount Power towards these States.

Part I.—page 25.

The deposition of Maharaja Pratap Singh in 1889—The 'edict of resignation'—The grounds of deposition—The incriminating letters—Brief refutation of those grounds—Col. Sir O. St. John on the reforms introduced by the Maharaja—Transfer of Sir Oliver a misfortune to Cashmere—Maharaja's conceptions of his duties—His letter to Lord Dufferin—His installation speech—Reforms initiated by him in first year of his reign—Harsh treatment of the Maharaja—An apology for the Government of India—The Maharaja not molested any further—Not taken into confidence—Sir O. St. John's successors—Reference to the Mahomedan subjects of the Maharaja deprecated—Dr.

Hunter on the subject—The Hindus beat the Mahomedans on their own ground—In India people cannot demand to be ruled by their co-religionists only—The mischievous policy of setting Hindus against Mahomedans—Its lamentable consequences—The Maharaja's kind and impartial treatment of his Hindu and Mahomedan subjects —His generosity towards the followers of other creeds—The Maharaja's feelings after his deposition—His letter to the Viceroy—The latter's reply—The Maharaja returns to Jummu in the middle of 1889—Lives in seclusion—His anxiety to meet the Viceroy—Difficulties in the way—A favourable turn—Col. Nisbet goes on furlough—Col. Prideaux appointed to the Residency—His conciliatory attitude towards the Maharaja—His speedy success—Delicate nature of a Residents' work—His position in the State where he is posted—Indian Princes how amenable to their influences—The way in which the Residents should conduct themselves—Their indiscretion leads to strained feelings—The necessity of exercising care in the selection of Residents—Princes should be allowed to lay their complaints direct to Government—Their shortcomings—Residents should act as their 'guide, friend and philosopher'—Improvement in the posture of the Maharaja's affairs soon after the appointment of Col. Prideaux—The Viceroy's proposal to visit Cashmere—His Excellency leaves Simla—Banquet at Srinagar and the Resident's speech—The Viceroy's reply—Kind assurances—Their effect on the public mind—The enquiries by the Viceroy—His interviews with the Maharaja—Result—Partial restoration of the Maharaja—a measure of justice.

Part II.—page 72.

Change in the Maharaja's position—Far from pleasant at first—His path strewn with thorns—He meets with opposition and is thwarted—Intrigues—His responsibilities—His powers inadequate for their proper discharge—Left to his own resources—His good nature and his good sense prevail—His kind treatment of his opponents—Valuable help and sympathetic attitude of Col. Prideaux—The Maharaja's visit to Lahore in March 1892—Cholera in Cashmere—Fires and scarcity—The Maharaja's anxiety to see his subjects—He is detained at Jummu—His solicitude—Relief measures ordered by him on a liberal scale—Medical aid—Pundit Suraj Kaul sent to Cashmere to provide against scarcity—His success—Grants to the sufferers from fire—Testimony of an Anglo-Indian paper—The Maharaja goes to Srinagar in July 1892—Visits Gulmarg—His attention engrossed in pressing affairs of State—Sanitary improvements in Srinagar—Water works proposed—The Maharaja's tender sympathy for the peasantry—Remission of large arrears of revenue—Announced at the Dusserah Durbar—Description of the Durbar—His subjects' attachment to the Maharaja—The Maharaja's speech—He divines good to his people from the fixity of the assessment—Wishes them peace and prosperity—The Maharaja's strong desire to ameliorate their condition—Mr. Wingate's testimony in His Highness's favour and against his officials—Conclusions from Mr. Wingate's testimony—Investiture of the Maharaja with the insignia of the Star of India—The Resident's speech—Address to the Maharaja by his subjects—Its value as shewing their sentiments towards him —The Maharaja returns to Jummu—Valedictory reception and entertainment to Lord Roberts—Their justification—High compliment paid by Lord Roberts to the Maharaja's loyalty and services—The Maharaja's capacity for sustained work—Lord Roberts' farewell entertainment at Lahore—The Maharaja joins it—His reasons—He wins golden opinions.

Part III.—page 114.

The Maharaja's reverses were not of his own seeking—were due to causes beyond his control—Mr. Plowden's recommendation to set aside the Maharaja

—rejected by Lord Dufferin in July 1888—His Lordship's advice to Mr. Plowden to proceed in a judicious and sympathetic spirit—Mr. Plowden's failure—His wrong estimate of the Maharaja—His remarks against Raja Amar Singh—Reforms initiated by the Maharaja in the first year of his reign—Causes of their defeat—Good work done by the Maharaja since his partial restoration—Land settlement and remission of arrears—Their beneficial effect—Accounts—The budget—Official integrity—The judicial and the executive—The laws of the State—Honorary Magistrates—Reclamation of waste lands—Roads and bridges—Sanitation and conservancy of Srinagar—Water-works—Schools—The *begar* cess—Restrictions on forced labour—The Mian Rajputs—Army organisation—Remission of arrears in the Military Department—Farm of customs duties—Purchase of State supplies and stores—The feudatories—The Mission Hospital—The Mastgurh Musjid—Religious toleration—Encouragement of letters—The above list satisfactory—Attitude of the Maharaja's brothers towards His Highness—The Hindu scriptures—The sons of Dasaratha—Their noble example—The Ramayana—Its lessons—Should not be lost upon royal brothers—Their loyalty to the Maharaja not only a matter of duty but also of self interest—The result of their past conduct—Byegones should be forgotten—Exhortation for more becoming conduct in future—Durbar at Jummu on 10th March 1893—Distribution of the Empress medals to the Maharaja's army—The Maharaja's speech—His expressions of loyalty—His advice to his soldiers—The concluding passage in his speech—The Maharaja's loyalty inherited—Maharaja Runbir Singh—His magnanimity—Services rendered by the Jummu family—At the annexation of the Punjab—In 1857—At the siege of Delhi and on other occasions—The Hazara expedition—The Yarkand Mission—Russia in Central Asia—The Agror Valley and Black Mountain expeditions—Recent operations on the frontiers—Outlay of money—Claims of the Maharaja upon the kindness and consideration of the British Government—Those claims not duly recognised—Examination of certain statements made against the Maharaja—Not correct that population in Cashmere 'had steadily dwindled'—Nor that the people had become 'impoverished to the point of chronic scarcity'—Nor that the Maharaja had no inclination to improve the condition of his people—Nor that he was incompetent to manage his affairs.

Conclusion—page 155.

The Maharaja the victim of misrepresentations—He submitted to his fate with patient dignity—He deserves ampler justice than has been meted out to him—Considerations in his favour—The treaty of Amritsar—Her Majesty's Proclamation of 1858—Misconceptions regarding the Maharaja—Appeal to His Excellency the Viceroy—Lord Cross's pledge in the House of Lords—It is time to redeem that pledge—Present condition of affairs—System of double government—The Maharaja's difficulties—He should be rescued from his present predicament—Expediency and justice as well as sound policy require it—The Resident cannot always help the Maharaja—The Maharaja's hands should be strengthened and he should receive sympathy and support—The Maharaja on his own failure—His selection of his own ministers a *sine qua non* for his success—The Maharaja solicited a trial upwards of 4 years ago—It should be granted to him—Concluding remarks.

PREFACE.

IN attempting, a second time, an exposition of the affairs of Cashmere, I have studiously kept clear of controversial matters as far as possible. My whole object has been to state plainly the just case of the Maharaja and to press it upon the attention of His Excellency the Viceroy. Keeping this object in view, I have put together a few facts and arguments which, I confidently hope, will meet with His Excellency's kind perusal and consideration. The Maharaja has suffered too long already, and it will redound to the lasting glory of Lord Lansdowne if, before leaving India, he reverses the doom with which His Highness was visited four years and a half ago. I trust I have been able to shew, in the course of these pages, that the Maharaja amply deserves its reversal.

As a loyal subject of the British Government, I cannot be indifferent to imperial interests with which the welfare of the country is indissolubly mixed. These interests must have precedence over every other consideration, but I am convinced that the reinstatement of the Maharaja will only serve to promote those interests instead of damaging them in any way. This conviction and the justice of the Maharaja's cause have emboldened me to write this 'vindication and appeal,' in the humble belief that my motive shall not be misconstrued and my modest labour shall not become futile and abortive.

CALCUTTA:
The 20th September 1893.

J. C. BOSE.

INTRODUCTION.

FOUR years ago, I wrote a small book on "Cashmere and its Prince," with the object of exposing the ungrounded nature of the attacks made against the Maharaja by his opponents, and of bringing to the notice of the highest authorities the true character of the *imbroglio* which had then recently taken place in his state. The politics of Cashmere have undergone considerable change since that book was written. The Maharaja, who was at that time a merely ornamental figure-head in his own territories, without any power to interfere in any of their affairs, has been since elevated to the Presidentship of his Council, whose deliberations he assists and shares in and, sometimes, even guides and controls. For this elevation, the Maharaja and his friends and well-wishers are indebted to His Excellency the Marquis of

Lansdowne, who gave proof of the nobility of his head and heart by rendering to the Maharaja an instalment of justice no sooner he came to know that His Highness had been grossly misrepresented to His Excellency, and found out by personal contact with the Maharaja and a careful local enquiry in his dominions that he was neither such a bad man nor such an oppressive ruler as he had been pictured to be. The Viceroy's visit to the Happy Valley, in October—November 1891, was thus fruitful of one very beneficial result : it dispelled the false notions that had been formed of the Maharaja and led to his partial restoration to the throne of his ancestors. But the restoration has been as yet but *partial*, the Maharaja being still in all important and many unimportant matters subject to the Resident's will, and it is due to Lord Lansdowne, who was misled into sanctioning his downfall, to render him ampler and more complete reparation before His Excellency leaves the country. The object of this little book is to place a number of facts and arguments before His Excellency, showing how the Maharaja deserves such reparation at His Excellency's hands.

If the Maharaja were a tyrannical or an oppressive ruler, I should have been the last to take up the pen in his favour, or say a word on his behalf. But aware as I am from personal knowledge of the good traits in his character—his goodness, his benevolence, his courtesy, his deep and earnest anxiety for the welfare and advancement of his subjects, I have been much pained at the underserved treatment he has received, and having had the honour to serve him in a high capacity though for a brief period, have regarded it my duty to defend him against the ungrounded, unjust and not unoften evil-minded aspersions of his open enemies and false friends. And the call of this duty has seemed to me all the more imperative, as I consider the question of the Maharaja's restoration to full powers possesses a wider significance than can be predicated of his individual case. The question involves not merely the narrower issue whether one individual is to be unjustly kept out of his rights, but also the much broader one, namely, whether a Christian Paramount Power, placed by Providence to rule over the destinies of this vast country, should tolerate any injustice to one of its most loyal and devoted feudatories, and thereby lower its prestige in the eyes of the public here and in Europe. I am fully pursuaded that the adoption of such a course cannot fail to be highly injurious to its interests in the long run; and thus impelled by loyalty on the one hand and by gratitude on the other, I make bold to write these pages, in hopes that they will contribute to advance the cause of righteousness and truth.

There is another potent consideration which has swayed me in pursuing the resolution I have proposed to myself. In common with many of my countrymen, I am an ardent well-wisher of the Native States, and feel convinced that, in the forward march of the Indian nation under *pax Britannica*, they are destined to play an important part. They possess a utility all their own, and it is impossible that the purposes they are intended to serve in the economy of this vast empire can be accomplished by any other agency. It is, therefore, in the interests of the British Government as well as of the people of India that these states should be preserved intact and their privileges respected as much as possible. I do not mean to contend that when an Indian Prince is oppressive and tyrannical and palpably misgoverns his people, the Paramount Power in the exercise of its overrule should not heed his conduct nor take no notice of it. By virtue of its very position and the responsibilities that rest upon it, the Paramount Power may, in such an instance, be justified in taking suitable action; but no interference of a radical nature should, I submit, be ordered till an extreme case is made out, not on mere *exparte* reports of its Political

Agents, but on due enquiry conducted on some intelligible principles of justice and fair play, in which the alleged offender may have at least a chance of a hearing. Such proceedings cannot fail to produce the double beneficial effect of reassuring our Princes and enhancing the durability and glory of the British Government.

It would be beyond the scope of this little book to dilate on the utility of the Native States, or the purposes they are capable of serving in the domain of modern Indian politics. Yet, when it is remembered what deep sympathy is felt for the welfare of these States throughout the country and what loud clamour of displeasure and indignation is evoked when any of their chiefs meet with undeserved treatment, a few words of explanation may not be regarded unnecessary. There was a time when the whole country from the Himalayas to the sea used to be governed by indigenous agency. With the advent of the Mahomedans, the agency changed in a few places for a time, but our Mahomedan conquerors soon took up their permanent abode in India, and their sons and sons' sons became children of the soil. Thus in a few generations they became merged in the general population, and, though much religious rancour prevailed at one time between them and their Hindu fellow-countrymen, they gradually got reconciled to each other and began to live on terms of amity and friendship. What was foreign agency at the commencement thus imperceptibly received a native mould, and was transformed into the general indigenous administrative machinery of the country. Most parts of India still continued to be governed by the Hindus, with central power in some notable instances in the hands of the Moslem Emperors of Delhi, or, when these were not strong enough, in the hands of powerful governors or refractory rulers of *subahs* or provinces; but it used to be an established order of things that Hindus often held the highest posts under Mahomedan kings and *vice versa*. With the English conquest of India, this order of things underwent a complete change. The major part of the country passed directly under British rule, which has hitherto employed a strictly foreign agency in carrying on the administration and has been very much foreign in its characteristics and incidents. Security of person and property was speedily established, but for a time all political advancement of the native population received a sudden and unprecedented check. Previous to 1833, a man of the world-wide reputation for learning and ability like Raja Ram Mohan Roy, who under native domination would have aspired to and perhaps reached the highest posts, could gain no higher dignity under the British Government than a District Collector's Sherishtadarship. Things have since undergone a change for the better and some native gentlemen have been promoted even to High Court judgships; yet it would lead to sheer disappointment to expect a Salar Jung or a Madhava Rao in British India.

One of the strongest reasons why the Native States are so fondly loved by the people is that these states still afford them careers which are shut out, and supply opportunities for the development of their administrative talents which are not available, within the pale of British jurisdiction. It is well known that circumstances contribute very largely to make up a man, and that these circumstances are in British India somewhat adverse to the growth and expansion of governing capacities among the native population. The peculiar nature of the relationship which the rulers and the ruled bear to each other in this country render it improbable that, at least for some time to come, the former will be in a position to entrust the more capable among the latter with responsible and independent administrative charges. We have had men of ability in the Subordinate Executive Service, but they are creatures of a stereotyped system and are so completely fettered by what is technically known as 'red-tapism,' that as a rule they cannot originate a single administrative measure capable of producing beneficial results to an appreciable extent. We have lately had a small number of native District Officers in some parts of the country; but their opportunities also are very limited, while the success which has almost invariably followed their appointment strongly refutes the theory that the Indians are unfit for superior administrative work, and clearly shews that with better opportunities they might develop talents which now lie unused and dormant.

Another reason why the Native States are highly regarded is that they are associated in the popular mind with recollections of the political independence that was once enjoyed, and form landmarks as it were of that ancient civilization whose traces are still visible amidst the wreck and *debris* of ages. In spite of the absence of those refined methods which distinguish the government in the British territories, the rule of the Native

Princes possesses one decided advantage in that it is more sympathetic and more in harmony with the ideas, thoughts and usages of the people. Native Courts again have been patrons of learned men and men of character and sanctity, and protectors of the arts, industries and manufactures of the country. It is too true, as Col. Torrens has remarked, that 'the demand for Cashmere shawls has dwindled in extent as British supremacy has spread northwards from Bengal Proper,' and the fall of Lucknow and Delhi has been almost the shawl-makers' 'last and bitterest blow.' And what is true of the shawl manufacture is true also of the manufacture of many other indigenous fabrics which once commanded universal admiration by the superiority of their texture and quality. They are still prized by our Princes and Chiefs, who, even in their decline, encourage directly or indirectly these and other arts and industries, which but for them would have probably died out of the country.

Native States again are the only centres round which true self-government on an appreciable scale is possible in the present political exigencies of the country. Indians had successfully governed themselves from remote antiquity, and the resuscitation of their self-governing capacities is a desideratum not only to themselves but also to their British rulers and masters. Hence a movement in this direction is visible throughout the Empire. The higher instincts of the people are to be preserved and even developed, and Britain's mission in India is not to extinguish every spark of generous ambition in the Indian breast, but to generate in it that vital warmth which will call forth latent powers and susceptibilities and enliven the capacity for organisation and discipline self-government imposes. The utility of the Native States as self-governing agencies is palpable, and I can do nothing better to support my position than quote the utterances of our present Viceroy on the subject. Speaking at the St. Andrew's Dinner on

30th November 1891, Lord Lansdowne, after referring to His Excellency's visit to Cashmere and a few other Native States, observed—'I dwell upon these facts because I regard it as a matter of first rate importance that the states in subordinate alliance with Her Majesty should be so governed that we need have no scruple in preserving for them the measure of independence which they at present enjoy. Not only would it be an act of injustice to deprive them of the privileges of self-government to which they are entitled, but it would, I am convinced, be a distinct misfortune to the Empire if these interesting remnants of indigenous rule were to be entirely effaced. * * * It is instructive both for the natives of this country and for Europeans, that the two kinds of Government should be in force side by side, and in the full view of public opinion. We are all of us fond of dwelling upon the necessity of decentralising our administration, and considering all the circumstances of India, I doubt whether there is any form of decentralisation more useful than that which leaves the domestic affairs of a large portion of the country to the management of its own people.' These pregnant remarks of His Excellency will find an echo in every reasonable mind. There are no doubt Native States and Native States, but it is in the interest of them all that, while they should enjoy perfect liberty in the management of their internal affairs, they should live and grow in the full light of enlightened public opinion. This would purify their atmosphere where it is infected and show, at the same time, that we can still boast of a Mysore, a Travancore and a Baroda, whose government, managed by able native rulers and administrators, may compare favourably when placed in juxtaposition with even British rule.

But there is one more consideration, as powerful as the others, in favour of the Native States and their continuance, and this consideration weighs equally with the people and the Paramount Power. Sentiments of loyalty and gratitude for numerous boons received as well as the instincts of self-interest and self-preservation alike prompt the people to desire the continuance of British rule under whose protecting ægis they have been making rapid marches towards prosperity and civilisation ; and bearing in mind the services rendered to it by the Native States, they wish as a means to an end, that these states should flourish and prosper. As for the Paramount Power, the help it has received from our Princes and Chiefs has been repeatedly acknowledged, but by none so forcibly as by that illustrious statesman who wielded the destinies of this Empire in the terrible crisis of 1857. The Native States had been ruthlessly broken up and absorbed during the preceding *regime*, and the terrible mutiny, which Lord Canning was called upon to face and to quell, has been imputed mainly to the discontent caused by Lord Dalhouse's policy of annexation. An almost eye-witness thus describes the situation.—'The decade preceding the revolt of the army had seen the British dominions largely extended by the absorption of the Native States. Oudh had been annexed because of the King's misrule. One after another the states of Satara, Jhansi and Nagpur had been treated as escheats. It is true that neither the doctrine of escheat nor the practice was new. But they had never been so logically or systematically enforced. The views of the Governor-General were well known. He believed that petty principalities, intervening within the British boundaries, might be made the means of annoyance to us, but could never be a source of strength. He expressed that advantage should be taken of every just opportunity to get rid of them by annexing them when there were no direct heirs. He had applied his principles to one of the largest states and had argued for them in the case of the oldest. No ruling chief felt secure for the future, and there arose general fear.'*

* Aitchison's Lord Lawrence pp. 134—135.

The Native States had been thus treated down to 1856, and the Indian Princes, filled with consternation, trembled on their thrones, uncertain as to who would be the next victim. Yet, when in the following year the fire broke out which involved the Empire in one mighty conflagration, these very Princes voluntarily came to the side of the Paramount Power and manfully stood there till the fire was completely subdued and extinguished. How many instances does history furnish of such generous repayment? Lord Canning fully realised the situation and appreciated the valuable services so rendered at such a crisis; and in the fulness of his gratitude described the Native States as break waters to the storm, which would otherwise have swept over the Empire in one great wave. 'The safety of our rule,' wrote he, 'is increased, not diminished, by the maintenance of Native Chiefs well affected to us...............And should the day come when India shall be threatened by an external enemy or when the interests of England elsewhere may require that her Eastern Empire shall incur more than ordinary risk, one of our best mainstays will be found in these Native States.' These words from such authority shew more forcibly than volumes of argument the usefulness of the Native States as valuable auxilliaries in times of trouble and as pillars of strength to support the Empire in cases of internal disorder or external aggression.

Lord Canning was not singular in his views about the Native States, nor were those views based solely on his overwhelming sense of gratitude for the services his government had, at a most critical time, received unasked from the Indian Princes. He looked at the question from the liberal standpoint of practical politics, and other eminent British statesmen have expressed similar views on diverse occasions. Lord Ellenborough, for instance, writing in 1853, when the tide of annexation may be said to have reached its height, observed—'I consider that in fact our Government is at the head of the system composed of Native States, and I would avoid what are called rightful occasions of appropriating those territories. On the contrary, I should be disposed as far as I could to maintain the Native States, and I am satisfied that their maintenance and the giving the subjects of these States the conviction that they are considered permanent parts of the general Government of India would naturally strengthen our authority.' Sir Charles Wood (Lord Halifax), on 26th. February 1863, referred to the Native States in the House of Commons in the following terms—'The House may dismiss at once all question of the annexation of territory. There are many reasons why I think we should not annex the Native States. It is for our advantage that such States should be left in India.' And Lord Cranborne, on 12th July 1866, speaking at Stainford, said—'Thirty years ago, the predominant idea with many English statesmen was that our interest in India consisted in extending our territory to the largest possible extent. To that annexation policy the terrible disaster of the mutiny of 1857 must to a large extent be ascribed. But as time has gone on, that desire of increased dominion which is the natural temptation of all powerful States has been overcome, and statesmen of all parties have arrived at the conclusion that we now hold in India pretty well as much as we can govern, and that we should be pursuing an unwise and dangerous policy if we tried to extend our borders or to lesson the permanence of these Native Rulers upon whose assistance we have so long relied.'

Pages might be filled with extracts like the above, but it is superfluous to do so. It will suffice to give a passage from a document, issued in a solemn and deliberate form, after a most perilous moment had been safely passed, by the very highest authority in the whole British

Empire – from the Royal Proclamation of 1858—the Magna Charta, as it has been called, of the Princes and people of India. The passage referred to runs as follows— 'We hereby announce to the Native Princes of India that all treaties and engagements made with them by or under the authority of the Honourable East India Company are by us accepted and will be scrupulously maintained ; and we look for the like observance on their part. We desire no extension of our present territorial possession ; and while we will permit no aggression upon our dominions or our rights to be attempted with impunity, we shall sanction no encroachment on those of others. We shall respect the rights, dignity and honour of Native Princes as our own ; and we desire that they, as well as our subjects, should enjoy that prosperity and that social advancement which can only be secured by internal peace and good government.'

Her Majesty the Queen Empress' gracious Proclamation and the declarations of successive statesmen have ensured to the Princes of India the safe and peaceable enjoyment of their possessions and rendered a direct encroachment upon their powers and privileges next to impossible. A tendency was shown sometime ago to treat the Proclamation as a dead letter—as a make-shift which was intended to serve a temporary political purpose, but which, having served that purpose, should not carry any binding force on succeeding statesmen and administrators. Happily for the good name of the British government and the British nation, such a tendency received no countenance, and it may be hoped and expected that the royal words of the Empress of India will continue to impose obligations upon the rulers of the country whose force neither time nor distance will affect or obliterate. The Indian Princes are as steadfast and firm in their friendship and fidelity as ever; and the voluntary offers of help which reached the Government of India a few years back when there was an inclination on the part of the Northern Bear to pounce upon 'the garden of Central Asia,' and the zeal and earnestness with which the formation of the Imperial Service corps has been promoted, clearly demonstrate that they are ready and prepared to assist the Paramount Power with all the resources at their command; should any assistance be necessary, as they did in the dark and troublous days of 1857. The Paramount Power would greatly enhance their warm adherence to its cause and knit closer their bonds of allegiance by treating them with the honour and courtesy which are unquestionably their due, and in shewing the same fastidious scrupulousness in dealing with their rights and privileges as with its own. They are the mainstays of the Empire and sincere friends and well-wishers of the Paramount Power, and they possess every right to claim from it that fair and candid treatment which is as far above the clap-traps of diplomacy as honesty is above tricking subterfuge or low deceit. The British government as Lord Paramount no doubt owes certain duties to their subjects, and when one of them cruelly oppresses the latter or misbehaves in a scandalous manner let him be corrected by all means; but let the correction be preceded by a fair enquiry and imparted in such proportion as may be commensurate to his offence and in such a way as not to rouse needless suspicions regarding the motives of the Paramount Power nor groundless apprehensions in respect of ulterior consequences.

PART I.

The temporary deposition of Maharaja Protap Singh of Jummu and Cashmere took place in April 1889. It was based upon an 'edict of resignation' which purported to delegate the ruling power to a council for a period of 5 years. The Maharaja had inserted certain stipulations in the edict favourable to himself, but these were declared 'inconvenient' by the Government of India; and as it would have been 'embarrassing' to agree to the edict as it stood, it was treated 'as a confession of incapacity for the rule of the state,' and the action against the Maharaja was sanctioned on 'general grounds.' *

These 'general grounds' may be summarised in the following words of His Excellency the Viceroy, who addressing the Maharaja said—'Your Highness is

---

* *Vide* letter of Government of India to the Secy. of State dated 3rd April 1889.

correct in expressing your belief that the action subsequently taken by my government was not justified merely by the disclosures contained in these letters.......
..............Notwithstanding the ample resources of your state, your treasury was empty, corruption and disorder prevailed in every department and in every office, Your Highness was still surrounded by low and unworthy favourites, and the continued misgovernment of your state was becoming every day a more serious source of anxiety.'*

The language here used with regard to the 'letters,' that is, the so-called treasonable correspondence which Col. Nisbet, considered such a lucky find for the purpose of encompassing the ruin of His Highness, would lead one to suppose that these letters had furnished some ground to the Government of India for adopting harsh and relentless proceedings against the Maharaja. But the subsequent declaration of Sir John

---

* *Vide* Viceroy's letter to the Maharaja dated the 21th June 1889.

Gorst, then Under-Secretary of State for India, on the occasion of the Cashmere debate in the House of Commons, places the matter beyond all possibility of doubt. Sir John Gorst is reported to have observed—'These letters, in spite of what the Honourable Member says, have never been treated by the Government of India as serious, nor have they been made the ground for the exclusion of the Maharaja from interference in the public affairs of Cashmere. They might never have been noticed had they not been accompanied by the resignation of his own accord of part of his power.'* This declaration is very reassuring, as it saves the Maharaja at any rate from the charge of faithlessness and disloyalty, which of all men he least deserves.

As for the 'general grounds' on which the action of the government of India against the Maharaja was sought to be justified, it would be bootless to enter

---

* Hansard's report of proceedings in the House of Commons, dated 3rd July 1890.

into a discussion of them at this place. The Government of India have already made some amends for their past treatment of the Maharaja, and the best course therefore would be to allow the dead past bury its dead as far as possible. It would suffice merely to observe briefly in respect of those grounds that the contention on the Maharaja's side was that he had never been personally extravagant nor had he squandered away the resources of the State ; that he had been ever solicitous to check corruption and disorder in every department of the administration ; that he had introduced a large number of beneficial reforms and, if nevertheless misgovernment existed in his state, that was because he never possessed free will to carry on the administration after the manner nearest his heart ; and that the favourites complained of were his domestic servants and family priest who never exercised any influence over nor possessed any connection with the affairs of his government.

It would serve no purpose to deny that

there was any oppression in Cashmere at the moment of the Maharaja's temporary deposition. But it was the remnant of such oppression as had come down from generation to generation, and had reached its climax near the termination of the Sikh rule in 1846. Since then, the pressure upon the people had been, to use Mr. Wingate's words, 'undoubtedly relaxed' and progress made even in the times of the Maharaja's predecessors.* Affairs became much improved on the accession of Maharaja Pratap Singh to the *guddee.* This is borne testimony to by Col. Sir O. St. John who, after recounting a number of obnoxious imposts or customs duties, abolished or mitigated by the Maharaja's proclamation, wrote on 27th. September 1885 to the Government of India as follows—'On the whole, the above constitute a valuable boon to the people, especially to the cultivating classes of Jummu, whose main grievances are now removed. Sensible relief is also given to

* Mr. Wingate's Cashmere Settlement Report.

the Cashmere peasant; but the artisans of the towns, whose needs are greater, gets nothing but a slight possible reduction in the price of fruit and vegetables.'*

The reforms introduced at the time Col. Sir Oliver speaks of were comparatively few. They constituted about a fourth of what were initiated during the next six months. And the whole body of reforms, introduced by the Maharaja in the first year of his reign, covered very extensive ground, and touched not merely the peasantry but the artisans also and, in fact, all ranks and classes of his subjects and every department of the administration. One may well wonder what would have been Sir Oliver's sympathy with the Maharaja's Government if he had been in Cashmere to witness the inauguration of the later and much more considerable instalment of reforms, and how glad he would have been to help on those reforms with all the weight of his personal authority. It was an evil day

* *Vide* Parliamentary Blue Book on Cashmere p. 13.

for Cashmere when Sir Oliver St. John was removed from the Cashmere Residency and Mr. Plowden was installed in his place. The cold indifference and supercilious attitude of Mr. Plowden frustrated all the Maharaja's plans of good administration—all his endeavours to make his territories, to use his own words, 'a model of a well governed state in alliance with the Government of India', and they relapsed once more into a condition of oppression and disorder.

The Maharaja had from the very beginning of his career an adequate conception of his duties as a ruler. Writing to Lord Dufferin so far back as 18th September 1885, he said—'I may submit to your Excellency that I am fully aware of the wise and benevolent principles which guide the supreme government of India in its relations with the Native States, and I have not the least doubt that your Excellency will estimate me not by the splendour of my court, nor by the pomp of my retinue, but by my conduct towards my subjects, and by the only standard of good government combined with sincere and active loyalty.'* Again in his installation speech, the Maharaja made the following declaration which deserves an attentive perusal—'I need not trouble you now with minute details of what I intend to do, but I think I can declare without committing myself to any particular measure the policy and the general principles that will guide me in the conduct of my affairs. I shall adopt such measures only as are calculated to secure to my subjects their greatest good and the fullest enjoyment of their rights and privileges, and shall conduct my administration so that the tiller of the soil will enjoy a fair share of the produce of his labour, and the manufacturer the fruit of his skill and industry, that every facility will be given to commerce by improving the means of communication and removing unnecessary and vexatious restrictions, that every encouragement will be offered

* Cashmere Blue Book pp. 12-13.

to get all the resources of the country properly developed, that ample provision will be made for the relief of the sick and the suffering, and that real merit and worth in my subjects will be recognised and fostered without any distinction of race or rank, creed or colour'. * During the first year of his reign, the Maharaja carried out to the very letter the terms of this declaration. He freely admitted that there had been numerous abuses in the administration, and applied himself vigorously to remove the same. He received at the beginning the friendly sympathy and support of Sir O. St. John, as has been pointed out, and it is quite probable that had Sir Oliver continued in the Residency, the history of recent events in Cashmere would have been different from what it has been. But the fates had ordained otherwise, and the result was extremely disastrous to the Maharaja and his interests.

One is forced to confess that the

* Cashmere Bluebook p. 15.

Government of India dealt very harshly with the Maharaja in condemning him on the *exparte* report of his antagonists. But allowance should be made for the peculiar predicament in which the Government of India had been placed. Col. Nisbet was believed to be friendly to the Maharaja, and when he too joined his predecessor in condemning His Highness, the Government of India were taken unawares. Lord Lansdowne was new to the country, quite unused to the methods that prevailed here. His Lordship was, therefore, easily misled by the misrepresentations that were dinned into his ears. He could not then conceive that it was possible for an English gentleman to abuse the privileges of his responsible office to such an extent as induced the Government of India thereafter to hold that it was better that Col. Nisbet should retire from the service than that he should return to the Residency in Cashmere.

But while the Government of India

had been cruel to the Maharaja so far that they condemned him unheard, they tried to mitigate the hardship of their sentence by saving him from further molestation. They had taken away his powers and privileges, and reduced him to a mere ornamental figure-head ; yet they showed him consideration so far that he was permitted 'to retain his rank and dignity as Chief of the State and receive from the State revenues an adequate, but not extravagant, allowance for the maintenance of his household and any other necessary expenditure.' * If the Maharaja received injustice at the hands of the Paramount Power, it was injustice tempered by mercy, for there was nothing to prevent his being subjected to worse treatment than was meted out to him. His position was perfectly helpless, and if the plot set on foot against him by the production of the forged treasonable correspondence had succeeded, he would have been dragged down to a depth of degradation and misery

* Cashmere Bluebook p. 24.

which can be better conceived than described.

What strikes one as strange in connection with all the proceedings that were adopted against the Maharaja is that, though there had been so much complaint against his rule, he should have hardly been taken into confidence. Lord Dufferin, no doubt, in his letters as well as orally when the Maharaja paid a visit to Calcutta in the cold season of 1885-86, desired His Highness to govern his State with justice and moderation, and to introduce the reforms that had been rendered necessary on account of the disorganised state of the administration during the late Maharaja's illness. His lordship also desired the Maharaja to rely upon his agent Col. Sir O. St. John, and to be guided by his advice in carrying out these reforms.* As long as Sir Oliver was in Cashmere, cordial terms existed between the Maharaja and the Resident, but with his transfer all

* *Vide* Lord Dufferin's letter to the Maharajah, dated 14th September 1885.

cordiality between the two came to an end, and there was thenceforward nothing but indistinct grumbling on the one side and vain attempts at conciliation on the other. If Sir Oliver's successors had communicated to the Maharaja in a frank, genial and friendly manner all that the Government of India expected him to do and helped him in doing it, no complaints could have been possible on either side. But, far from this, the Maharaja was treated with haughteur or distrust, he was not consulted, he was opposed and thwarted, and in the end he was reported unfit to govern. The pursuit of a more reasonable course would have saved the Maharaja much needless humiliation, and the Government of India much obloquy for having sanctioned it.

There is one observation I should like to make at this place before proceeding with my narrative. It is a matter of the most sincere regret that, in dealing with the affairs of Cashmere, a discussion should have been introduced which could not fail to arouse ill-feeling between the Maharaja and his subjects. The Government of India were careful in their communications to the Maharaja not to lay stress upon the fact that he, a Hindu Prince, was ruling a Mahomedan population, nor draw any conclusions adverse to him on that ground. But Sir John Gorst, then Under-Secretary of State for India, in his speech in the Cashmere debate in the House of Commons in 1890, placed an undue emphasis upon it. He said—'It may indeed be questioned whether, having regard to the circumstances under which a Hindu family were settled as rulers, the intervention of the British Government on behalf of the Mahomedan people had not been already too long delayed.'* Sir John thus pleaded the cause of the Moslem cultivators against their Hindu ruler. This was very unfortunate and quite unworthy of the high dignitory who was expounding the case for the Government. Dr. Hunter was right when he asked—

*Hansard's report of the debate.

'Why the Moslem cultivator? Surely, a 'Hindu, if he happens to be a cultivator, is as much entitled to sympathy as the Moslem. But the right hon. gentleman laid stress on the word Moslem, in order to excite those unhappy religious prejudices which unfortunately prevail in India. We know that in India, unhappily, both Moslems and Hindus are animated by strong fanatical opinions, on the subject of religion, leading to collisions and breaches of the peace. And here is the Under-Secretary of State for India in this house pointing his moral by the contrast between the Moslem and the Hindu peasants, and trying thus to fan the embers of religious antipathy.'*

Every sensible and right-thinking man will endorse Dr. Hunter's opinion and feel regret that Sir John Gorst should have been betrayed into touching on such a delicate and difficult matter. Besides, it should be remembered that Mahomedan rule in Cashmere had terminated at least

*Hansard's report of the debate.

a quarter of century previous to its transfer to Maharaja Golab Sing. He took over possession of that province not from its Moslem rulers, but from the Governor who was holding it on behalf of the Sikh Durbar at Lahore. It should also be remembered that for some years previous to the treaty of Amritsar (1846) by which Cashmere was sold to him, he had been holding possession of the territories of Jummu, Ladakh and Baltistan in absolute sway, and the provinces of Cashmere and Gilgit alone were ceded to him by that treaty for a splendid valuable consideration. When Sir John Gorst spoke of the Maharaja of Cashmere, he meant not the Chief of the Cashmere Valley, but of the whole tract of country under his rule, with a total area of about 68,000 square miles, of which the Valley formed but the seventeenth part. His argument was, therefore, quite illogical and calculated to produce misconception. Somewhat akin to the argument advanced by the Ex-Under-Secretary of State for

India is the complaint, not unoften heard even from responsible parties, that most of the officials in Cashmere are Hindus. Those who give utterance to this complaint forget, or do not care to remember, that the Cashmeri Hindus, known by the name of Pandits or 'learned', are a lettered community, while the bulk of the Mahomedan population is perfectly illiterate. Persian is the court language in Cashmere, and here at any rate it might be thought that the Mahomedans possessed a decided advantage over the Hindus, but notwithstanding this advantage the Hindus by their assiduity beat the Mahomedans even on their own ground and push themselves forward. The most mediocre intellect might be prepared to admit that neither the Maharaja nor the Cashmeri Hindus deserved any condemnation on this account.

The objection that is sometimes brought forward to the domination of a Hindu Prince over Mahomedan subjects in Cashmere will, on a little examination, be found to be entirely fallacious and misleading. In the first place, whatever the reason, the Hindus have been governing Cashmere for nearly three quarters of a century, and the Mahomedans of Cashmere, most of whom are descendents of Hindu ancestors, have become fully reconciled to Hindu rule. The objection referred to can, therefore, only result in teaching the Cashmeri Mahomedan disrespect for constituted authority. Secondly, if the principle that co-religionists alone should rule over subjects professing a certain creed were enforced, what revolutions would come over India and what dire consequences would ensue? Thirdly, if in Cashmere proper the majority of the people are Mahomedans, (the same cannot be said of the richer and more populous province of Jummu), so in the Nizam's dominions the bulk of the population consists of Hindus. Would any one on that ground advance the proposal that the Nizam should cease to rule over the Deccan? If there be misgovernment in a

State, let it be condemned by all means, but let not the plea of misgovernment serve as an occasion for exciting the worst passions of denominational fanaticism and jealousy.

Men are not wanting who consider it not only an innocent, but a profitable, pastime to avail of every opportunity to set the Hindus and the Mahomedans by the ear, in as much as in their opinion it helps to perpetuate those antipathies that prevent the fusion of the Indian people into one nation. But these are clearly very short-sighted speculators who confine their range of vision within narrow limits. A little reflection should bring home to their minds the mischief these antipathies have been working to the country. Hardly a year passes without our hearing of some turbulent and murderous riots, in one province or another, between Hindus and Mahomedans, who 20 years ago were living on terms of harmony and good-will, and these riots have this year assumed unprecedented proportions. Whatever self-seeking politicians may think on the subject, it is the duty of every sincere well-wisher of the empire to try to soothe and conciliate these antipathies and restore amicable feelings between the two great sections of the Indian community.

As for the Maharajas of Cashmere, it may be stated without fear of contradiction that, from the days of Golab Singh, the Princes of the ruling dynasty have made little distinction between the two classes of their subjects. Whatever good or bad government has existed has been shared by both. The favours and disfavours of the governing authorities have fallen to the lot of the Hindu as well as of the Mahomedan cultivator. If there have been more Hindu than Mahomedan officials in the state, that is due to the fact, noticed before, that the Hindus in Cashmere are much more cultured than the Mahomedans. Yet it cannot be urged that Mahomedans have not often reached high positions of trust and responsibility. And if the Princes have been thus far impartial, they have been requitted by the zealous loyalty of their subjects of both creeds, who have vied with one another in shewing towards them their devotion, respect and attachment.

With regard to Maharaja Pratap Singh, it cannot for a moment be alleged that he has been guilty of a single act of unkindness towards the Mahomedans. Though a rigid Hindu himself in his belief and practices, he is tolerant of the faith of other people, and his open-handedness to the professors of other religions has been amply proved on several occasions. As instances, I may mention his liberality to the Catholic Missions at Baramula and Leh and the Catholic orphanage at Murree, his generous support to the Protestant Missionaries in Cashmere, and his restoration of the mosque at Srinagar, long lost to the Mahomedans, to the followers of Islam. It may not be out of place to state in this connection that, on 30th October 1891, a respectable deputation was sent by His Holiness the Pope to the Maharaja, in recognition of the latter's marked liberality towards the Church of Rome. The deputation consisted of Father Brown, Prefect Apostolic, and Fathers Winkley and Cunningham, who presented the Pope's letter and a mosaic representing the Domo of Palermo to His Highness. It was, therefore, nothing short of a grievous wrong and injustice to the Maharaja to insinuate that, as a Hindu Prince, he could ever be guilty of or tolerate an act of unkindness and oppression towards any classes of his subjects, simply because these happened to profess a creed different from his own.

I have already adverted to the fact that Maharaja Pratap Singh was temporarily deposed in April 1889, and also briefly to the grounds on which his deposition was based. The Maharaja was at that time in Cashmere and, as might be expected, in a very miserable state of mind. The exultations of his enemies on his downfall added poignancy to his feelings and almost completed the cup of his misery. Writing to Lord Lansdowne shortly afterwards, the Maharaja observed —'They (his enemies) are now full conquerors over me and trample me under foot. What is my position now?—Simply that of a dead body ;—even worse than that, for I am taunted every moment by some sort of disgrace or disregard or other ; those inferiors and traitors who only yesterday shewed me every respect and bowed down before me, pass me now with contemptuous smile, and I constantly bear the destruction and degradation of all these my faithful and old servants who stood by me—of course, a dead body is unconscious of all these troubles of which unfortunately I am not.' * These sentiments were expressed in a lengthy and well-reasoned letter, which entered a respectful yet emphatic protest against the one-sided proceedings that had been adopted against him. The letter, moreover, was a correct exposition of the machinations by

* Maharaja's letter to the Viceroy, dated 14th May 1889.

which his opponents had triumphed over him, and a moving appeal to His Excellency the Viceroy to grant him the justice to which, as a faithful and devoted ally and a perfectly innocent man, he was entitled. Lord Lansdowne, on 29th June 1889, wrote a sympathetic reply to the Maharaja, but His Excellency did not admit the arguments put forward by the Maharaja in his own favour. His Excellency briefly described the circumstances under which the decision of the Government of India, sanctioning His Highness's temporary deposition, had been arrived at, contradicted the arguments advanced by him, and informed him that the control of affairs could not any further be left in his hands, exhorting him at the sametime to bear his loss of power in a dignified manner.'*

Before this reply was addressed to the Maharaja, he had left Cashmere and returned to Jummu, though the Council of State was still sojourning at Srinagar.

* Cashmere Blue Book p. 35 *et. seq.*

The contumelious behaviour of his servants and subordinates forced him to this course. He found that life was to him entirely unsupportable among the to him now painful surroundings of the 'Happy Valley.' The Resident remonstrated with the Maharaja for hurrying away from his summer capital, but he had been too much grieved to listen to such remonstrances. He hastened back to his ancestral home and shut himself up in his palace, thereby avoiding the taunts and insults of his exulting opponents. But though to avoid the dishonour that had been heaped upon his head, he thus far acted against the wishes of the Resident, he in other respects submitted to his reverses with a calm dignity, relying on the righteousness of his cause and confiding in the sense of justice of the Paramount Power. He was conscious that he had become the victim of misrepresentations, and felt convinced that no sooner Lord Lansdowne came to know the true facts of his case than His Excellency would try to reverse the doom that had been passed upon him. And he was right as the subsequent course of events has amply shewn.

The Maharaja, therefore, though bearing his adversity with patience and fortitude, naturally felt anxious to have a meeting with the Viceroy, as the best and surest means of dispelling the false notions that had been propagated against him. He was under the impression, and very rightly, that a few minutes' conversation with Lord Lansdowne would satisfy the latter that he was far other than he had been represented to be. And this impression gained ground with him in consequence of the concluding words of His Excellency's reply to the Maharaja's letter, dated 29th June 1889, referred to above, wherein His Excellency said—'I shall at any convenient time be ready to receive you and converse with you in a friendly and confidential spirit.'

But though the Maharaja was thus anxious to come into personal contact with the Viceroy, and though His Excellency was willing to give him a friendly reception and audience, much difficulty was experienced in bringing about an interview on account of the hostile attitude which the Resident had taken up against him. He himself did not wish to ask the good offices of Col. Nisbet in the matter, nor could Lord Lansdowne desire that he should be escorted to His Excellency by the very man who, under the garb of a friend, had been the immediate cause of his ruin. Such a course would have been undesirable on other grounds too, and would have had the sure effect of frustrating to a great extent the object of the interview. And yet it would have been against etiquette and established usage for the Maharaja to visit the Viceroy, except in the Company of some responsible British officer. The Maharaja was consequently in a fix and quite undecided as to what he should do, when events took a turn which helped the solution of his difficulty.

Col. Nisbet went, or was sent, on furlough in the cold season of 1890-91. It seems as if the Government of India had been able to perceive that he had overdone his work, and thereby marred his own reputation and soiled the good name of the Paramount Power, and as if they, therefore, availed of the earliest opportunity to move him out of the sphere of mischief. The Indian public could not readily believe that an autocrat, who had given up a first grade Commissionership in the Punjab to take up, on 25 per cent less emoluments, the Residency in a Native State, for the sake of the powers and prerogatives attached to it, would be in a hurry to forego the exercise of authority of which he was so devotedly fond, even for the pleasures of a sojourn at home. But whatever the cause may have been, and it is needless to enquire into it for my present purposes, the fact remains that he left Cashmere for England never to return to his post, and was succeeded by Col. Prideaux, late British agent at the court of the deceased Ex-King of Oudh.

This was a very fortunate event for the Maharaja and the State of Cashmere. Col. Prideaux had had in his dealings with the late Wajid Ali Shah won general respect and confidence, and a change for the better became noticeable in the affairs of the Maharaja soon after his installation into the Cashmere Residency. The powerful intrigues against His Highness that had poisoned thc atmosphere of Cashmere received an unexpected check, and he was rescued from the contumacious surroundings which had cmbittered his existence during the preceding *regime.* The relations between the Resident and the Maharaja also underwent considerable improvement on Col. Prideaux assumming charge of his office. The coldness and distance, that had characterised their mutual intercourse in his predecessor's time, disappeared and were replaced by good feeling and cordiality. Within three months of his appointment, Col. Prideaux began to make a mark and win golden opinions from those who came in contact with him. Gentle and yet firm, kind, courteous and considerate, he acquired more influence by his tact and affability in a couple of months than Col. Nisbet, with all his hectoring and bluster, had been able to gain in as many years. It soon became apparent that Col. Prideaux was the right man in the right place. The concerns of the state had lapsed into utter confusion owing to the mismanagement that had prevailed during the preceding incumbency ; the Prince himself had been ruthlessly discredited, degraded and dishonoured ; and the polity had received numerous rents and holes which caused wide-spread pain and misery. Col. Prideaux was deputed to remedy this state of things, and it redounds highly to his credit that he acquitted himself well within a brief period. He possessed an adequate conception of the difficulties and of the duties, functions, and responsibilities of his new office, and having both a head and a heart, achieved speedier success than had been looked for.

The task which a Resident in the Court of an Indian Prince has to perform is of a delicate nature and requires careful handling. He has to hold the scales, as it were, between the Paramount power whose accredited agent he is, on the one hand, and the Prince to whose Court he is deputed, on the other. While the Paramount Power reposes unbounded confidence in him, he is looked up to by the Prince with respectful attention as a mediator and an arbiter of his fate. The Resident has, therefore, to exercise much judgment, firmness and moderation to perform his allotted task in a satisfactory manner. The interests of the Paramount Power require that its Agents should, instead of lording over them, deal with its feudatories in a benignant and sympathetic spirit, and thus tie them closer to its side in bonds of gratitude and affection. When therefore a Resident behaves towards a Prince in an exacting and supercilious manner, he injures the interests of his employer, and renders himself practically useless as regards the discharge of many a duty and function attached to his office.

Indian Princes, whatever else their shortcomings, are seldom destitute of that politeness and courtesy that characterize all Indian noblemen and gentlemen. They may not often distinguish themselves in these days by marked intellectual powers, but few of them are devoid of the milder qualities of the heart. As a rule, they are remarkably susceptible to influences when these are exerted in a just, reasonable and wholesome manner; and in the case of the Resident, these influences become far more potent and operative, he being the trusted officer of the Paramount Power upon whose kindness and good opinion they set such a high value. It only requires some temper and patience and a little self-sacrifice on the part of the Resident to make a Prince completely amenable to his influences. Indian Princes, as Princes elsewhere, may be excused for cherishing an idea of their own importance and of the dignity and privileges attached to their rank and station. It is natural on their part to expect that those who come in contact with them should deal with them in a fair, decent and gentlemanly way. A Resident who does this and shews them the respect and consideration due to their position, gains an ascendancy over them in a short time ; but when he pursues an opposite course, as did Col. Nisbet in Cashmere, there result irritation, and-mutual distrust and ill-feeling, and all those deplorable consequences that have been witnessed in that unfortunate state.

No doubt in all contests between the British Agent and the Indian Prince, the latter, as by far the weaker of the two, has necessarily to go to the wall. The Government of India consider themselves pledged to support their own officer, especially as they generally listen to one side of the story, the Prince's version seldom reaching them. According to official rules, the Prince must submit his complaints against the Agent through that Agent himself, and it may not be judging the Agent too harshly to say that he feels disposed at times to take advantage of his position. Thus strained feelings arise, and though the Indian Princes are loyal to the back-bone, considerable discontent is nevertheless sometimes generated in their minds, and they chafe and murmur and find some difficulty in reconciling themselves to their lot.

It may be at once conceded that the mental equilibrium of the Paramount Power cannot be disturbed by the insignificant resentment of the Princes. Yet it is opposed to sound policy to rouse their discontent, or to afford room for the impression that their faithful devotion is not adequately recognised nor properly requited. I have already dwelt upon their value and usefulness as friends and allies, and it will suffice to observe here that, considering the yeoman's services they have done and are again likely to do, they have every right to claim a generous and honorable treatment at the hands of the Paramount Power. The best way to ensure this treatment is to depute such officers to their courts as may be possessed of tact and temper, of genial manners and a conciliatory disposition. Instructions might also, I submit, be given to these officers not to domineer over them, and some supervision might be maintained over the conduct of these officers themselves, so that they might not be tempted to overstep the limits of decorum and propriety. This last could easily be effected by allowing greater facilities to the Princes to lay their grievances before the Government of India. The apprehension that in such a case the Government would be deluged with petitions from these Prince is not well-founded, for the Agents of the Government are held in awe in the courts of the Princes, and the latter would never think of complaining against the former, unless actually goaded to such a course by intolerable high-handedness and oppression.

Nor can there be any ground for the apprehension that the prestige of the Government would suffer in any way for checking the vagaries of their Agents. It would rather immensely increase, as it consists more in a superior sense of right and justice than in brute force, more in moral predominance than in the power of powder and steel; and it may be respectfully pointed out that one instance of an erring Agent brought to judgment would raise the Government higher in the public estimation and render it more permanant good, than the *exparte* condemnation of ten of the highest Princes in the land.

The rule of these Princes is no doubt not always *sans reproche*. But is not the British Agent expected to act as their 'guide friend and philosopher,' and gradually to lead and help them on to reformed methods of administration? It is his duty not only to watch the interests of his Principal in their Courts, but also to further their interests with his enlightened and sympathetic counsel, and to act as mediator between them and the Paramount Power. It is within his power to turn himself into an effective engine of beneficence to myriads, nay millions, of human beings, if he only chooses to be true to his position, to act with considerateness, honesty and self-control, and to treat the Princes with friendliness and confidence.

But to return : I have already referred to the appointment of Col. Prideaux to the Residency in Cashmere. Shortly after his arrival, he began his work of benevolence by trying to throw oil upon troubled waters, and allaying irritation as far as was possible under the circumstances. He soon acquired an influence over the Durbar, and the Maharaja, finding him well-disposed, began to repose confidence in him. Thus the difficulty that had been felt about arranging a meeting of the Maharaja with the Viceroy gradually disappeared, and negotiations on the subject began to progress from day to day. The idea at first was that the Maharaja should come to Simla where the Viceroy was staying, but this idea was subsequently abandoned, and His Excellency conceived the generous plan of personally going to Cashmere to examine with his own eyes the posture of affairs, and to decide for himself, after a careful local enquiry, what course in respect of the Maharaja should be pursued in future.

The proposal of the Viceroy's visit to Cashmere, as it became known, gave rise to considerable speculation as regards the object of the visit. The more pronounced journals of Anglo-Indian opinion assured the public that there was no room for the apprehension that the Maharaja would meet with any measure of justice at the hands of His Excellency, that things would be maintained in their *status quo ante,* and that the policy that had been pursued would receive a further confirmation. The organs of Native opinion, on the other hand, predicted from the proposed visit good fortune for the Maharaja and his people. They argued that the Viceroy had been new to the country when the *imbroglio* in Cashmere had taken place, that he had subsequently come to know the true facts of the case, and that he would in all probability make reparation to the Maharaja for the injustice that had been done to him. The sequel showed that the former were wrong, and that the anticipations of the latter were not unfounded.

The Viceroy left Simla for Cashmere on 14th October 1889. Ample preparations had been made for His Excellency's reception, and his entry into the 'Happy Valley' was signalised by an amount of demonstration worthy of the occasion. On the 16th October, His Excellency's camp reached Murree where he made a stay of three days. The journey from Murree to Srinagar, performed partly by *tonga* and partly by boat, occupied five days. The Maharaja, with the Resident and the members of the Council and other dignitories, received His Excellency at a certain distance from the city down the river, where a State procession of boats was formed and moved up to Srinagar. On the 24th, official visits were exchanged between the Viceroy and the Maharaja, the two being for the first time brought face to face, and in the evening His Highness entertained Lord Lansdowne and party at a State banquet at the Lalmandi Palace to which a large number of guests had been invited. After dinner, the Maharaja entered and took his seat to the right of the Viceroy. Col. Prideaux then rose and, on the Maharaja's behalf, proposed the health of Her Majesty the Queen Empress. He next proposed the toast of Lord and Lady Lansdowne, emphasising, in the course of his speech, the Maharaja's desire that the Viceroy should visit his State. He said—'I have been commissioned by His Highness the Maharaja to express the great gratification he feels at the visit which their Excellencies the Viceroy and Lady Lansdowne have paid to his capital. It has been a long-cherished desire on the part of His Highness that the Viceroy should visit Cashmere as his guest, and I am extremely thankful to say that that desire is now fulfilled and that His Highness's wishes have been realised.'

Lord Lansdowne's reply was suitable and couched in language full of sympathy for the Maharaja. In the course of it, His Excellency remarked—'Your Highness, anxious as I was to visit your State, it was certainly not merely with the object of seeing its great natural beauties that I undertook my present tour. If I had been coming here merely as a tourist, I should have regarded my visit with much less interest than that which I feel in it at the present moment. It is not necessary for me to remind Your Highness that, almost from the time of my arrival in India, the affairs of Cashmere have constantly engaged my thoughts. The principal cause of my anxiety not to postpone my visit to you was the desire which I felt to make your personal acquaintance, a desire which I am glad to think was reciprocated by you, and to effect a full and frank intercharge of ideas with you upon matters of interest to us both.'

Then, after mentioning that the discussion of important questions connected with the government of Cashmere had been already receiving His Excellency's attention, the Viceroy proceeded—'Your Highness may depend upon it that I shall approach the consideration of these questions, in which you are so deeply interested, with feelings entirely friendly towards your Highness. I am, indeed, glad to be able, on this interesting occasion, to assure your Highness publicly, as I have already done in my private communications, that the Government of India has, throughout, entertained towards Your Highness and towards the Cashmere State, no sentiments other than those of sincere good will and sympathy, coupled with an earnest desire to assist you in surmounting the many difficulties and in bearing the heavy load of responsibilities with which you have been confronted, I trust the assurance which I am thus able to give Your Highness will dispel once and for ever the mistaken idea that, in its dealings with the Cashmere State, the Government of India harbour for a moment any ulterior designs upon its rights and privileges.'

The assurance, thus solemnly given on such an important occasion, served to disabuse the public mind of the erroneous notion that had been formed of the object the Paramount Power had in view in deposing the Maharaja. The deposition had taken place without any warning, under circumstances which looked rather suspicious. The Resident's action in wresting the so-called 'edict of resignation' from the Maharaja possessed all the appearance of a *coup*, and the hasty decision of the Government of India clothed it with a worse aspect. The Maharaja had been denied the right of self-defence, granted even to the meanest of Her Majesty's subjects, and summarily deprived of his most valued rights and privileges. The whole of India had naturally become convulsed in one fit of excitement at the apparently cruel and unjust treatment which the all-powerful Government had dealt out, on the one-sided report of a Political officer, to a most faithful, loyal and devoted feudatory, the first Prince in Northern India, one of the natural leaders of the hundred and fifty millions of Arya Varta. The Princes and Chiefs in other parts of India had regarded the act of the Government with surprise, sorrow and concern, and people had been heard to ask in wonder and suspense whether the days of annexation were going to be revived. Considerable unrest had prevailed in consequence, and the Viceroy's assurance was, therefore, given not a day too early; and, followed as it was a few days later by the announcement that the Maharaja had been installed into the Presidentship of his Council, it soothed the public mind and restored confidence in the good faith and honesty of purpose of the Supreme Government.

The Viceroy, during his stay in Cashmere, instituted a thorough enquiry into the state of affairs and had frequent interviews with the Maharaja. The result of this enquiry and these interviews was the partial restoration of the Maharaja, to which I have already referred. The Viceroy, in his speech at the St. Andrew's Dinner in Calcutta a few weeks later, referred to this act of kindness and justice in the following words—'My longest visit was that which I paid to the state of Cashmere. And, Gentlemen, I must express the pleasure which it gave me, after a very careful enquiry into its affairs, to be able to invite His Highness the Maharaja once more to take part in the Government of the State, of which we have never ceased to regard him as the legitimate ruler.' This statement of the Viceroy was exceedingly satisfactory. It finally disposed of the insensate and prejudiced clamour against the Maharaja's fitness to rule his State, and proved to the world that the charge of incompetency brought against him was without a foundation. Two successive Residents had pronounced distinctly and strongly against him, yet a 'very careful' local enquiry convinced the head of the Indian Government that the Maharaja, who had been only a short time before set aside as entirely worthless, deserved to be invited once more to take part in the Government of his State. Neither Mr. Plowden nor Col. Nisbet could discover any redeeming traits in the Maharaja's character ; but Lord Lansdowne, as soon as he came into personal contact with His Highness, and had an opportunity of ascertaining the facts of his case, saw through the veil of misrepresentations that had shrouded the truth from His Lordship, and he lost no time to render the Maharaja such reparation as under the circumstances he could do, without stultifying the previous conduct of the Government of India. This action of Lord Lansdowne was all the more welcome, in as much as it was no return for the splendid hospitality with which he had been received by the Maharaja, but was the result of a 'very careful enquiry' and, therefore, a measure of justice which His Lordship must have considered was the Maharaja's due.

PART II.

THE events just chronicled took place in Cashmere in November 1891. A few days later, the Maharaja returned to Jummu. He had been deposed in April 1889, so nearly two years and a half had expired before his partial restoration by Lord Lansdowne. During all this period, the Maharaja had had no hand in the administration of his own territories, but had passed his time merely as an on-looker, fretting and chafing at the affronts and indignities which his opponents had never missed an opportunity to heap upon him. A born Prince and the rightful ruler of his state, his position could not have failed to be most galling to him, however much he might have tried to keep up appearances and maintain an attitude of composure and dignity. But he was no longer a mere spectator, but was now an actual participator in the cares of state, and the seclusion by which he had hitherto avoided his enemies was no longer possible for him.

The Maharaja on his arrival at Jummu, found that his new position was far from pleasant to him. Those who had expected to profit by betraying his interests and combining to bring about his ruin, were greatly disappointed at the turn affairs had taken. They had hoped to be rewarded for their faithlessness and treachery, and were taken unawares at the Maharaja's partial restoration. It came as a surprise upon them, and for a time they could not brook the idea that the man who had fallen under their conspiracy should rule over them again. The Maharaja's path was therefore strewn with thorns. His opponents were many and powerful, and though they had been somewhat awed by the recent action of the Viceroy, it would have been too much to expect that they should submit quietly to his authority upon whose fall they had built hopes of their own advancement and prosperity.

The Maharaja's position at this time was quite anomalous indeed. A sovereign Prince, unceremoniously set aside and excluded a short time ago from the government of his own territories, he was reinvested with but limited authority and made President of his Council. In this capacity, he was required to act in concert with men whose interests were inconsistent with his own, and whom he possessed no authority to keep in proper subordination and under due control. They owed him no obligation and did not consider themselves bound to him by any ties of allegiance. They were quite unwilling, therefore, to shew him the respect and pay him the obedience due to his rank and dignity. They rather tried to oppose and thwart him, and intrigue consequently again raised its head to an unprecedented height.

These were some of the Maharaja's difficulties, but not all. As President of the Council, he was placed on his trial as it were, with expectations that he would come successful out of it. But though heavy responsibilities thus attached to his new dignity, he did not possess powers commensurate to those responsibilities, nor had he men about him who could give him wise counsel or help him out of the complications by which he was beset. Amid the clash of contending interests, the machinations of self-seeking covetousness, and the stir of unscrupulous ambition, the Maharaja was left entirely to his own resources to rescue himself, as well as he could, from the difficult position in which circumstances had placed him.

If the Maharaja had been as weak as he had been depicted to be, he would have undoubtedly succumbed under the load of his difficulties. He had been very miserable before his restoration, but he had had no responsibilities to discharge then nor any functions to perform, and the eyes of all had been not turned towards him to see how he acquitted himself. He had been living in retirement and privacy, apart from the din and turmoil of the world, performing his devotions and doing the little acts of charity and kindness for which opportunity had been still left to him. But now his predicament became altogether different. His good name as a ruler had been spoilt, he had been grossly maligned and misrepresented, and the falsest rumours had been circulated against him. The Viceroy after a 'very careful enquiry' formed an opinion favourable to the Maharaja, and though he did not reverse his former order, he considerably modified it. The Maharaja was drawn out from his seclusion, and placed in the full gaze of public opinion to prove his capacities as a ruler. But the obstacles in the path of his success were varied and numerous, and he would have stumbled across another failure if he had been hasty, impatient or cross.

Under such circumstances, the Maharaja's innate good nature and his good sense came to his rescue. He bore all opposition with patience and temper, and adopted a dignified and conciliatory demeanour even towards his bitterest opponents. He had kind words even for those who had been instrumental in bringing about his downfall. Thus, by a mixture of firmness and leniency, he gradually succeeded in disarming opposition and dulling the edge of intrigue. He could not, however, have succeeded in doing this, had he not been supported and helped by the Resident. Col. Prideaux's friendly and sympathetic attitude towards the Maharaja at this time deserves all praise. It was chiefly through his advice and assistance that he gradually recovered his position, asserted and maintained his dignity, and discomfitted those opponents who looked upon his restoration with feelings of resentment and jealousy.

In March 1892, the Maharaja paid a visit to Lahore. His ostensible object was to bid farewell to Sir James Lyall, a friend and well-wisher of his, and welcome Sir D. Fitzpatrick as new Lieutenant Governor of the Punjab. He had also another object in view. He is fully conscious that the rulers of Native States cannot but be gainers by coming in frequent contact with the British system of administration. Though not desirable that that system should be introduced in Native States in all its integrity, it furnishes a good model by following which the government of those states may be considerably benefitted and improved. The Maharaja accordingly stayed for more than a week at Lahore, and fully utilized his stay, although suffering from ill-health, in visiting the Chief Court and other public institutions in the capital of the Punjab, and gathering useful and practical information regarding the details of administration in a British province.

Col. Prideaux left for Cashmere in April 1892. Shortly afterwards, cholera of a most virulent type broke out there. The ravages of the fell disease went on rapidly increasing, till within a few weeks it assumed dreadful epidemic proportions, the number of attacks in the city of Srinagar alone reaching the appalling figure of 500 a day. The whole place was in a scare. Thousands of souls were carried away in a couple of months. A terrible fire also broke out about this time, and reduced a considerable portion of Srinagar into ashes. But as if these scourges were not sufficient, a scarcity made its appearance and completed the miseries of the people.

The Maharaja, on hearing of the outbreak of cholera, became impatient to start for Cashmere, and his impatience increased as harrowing reports of the sufferings of his subjects began to reach him. But Col. Prideaux, who had retired to Gulmarg on the appearance of the epidemic in the Valley, was too anxious for the personal safety of the Maharaja, and strongly objected to his visiting the scene of danger. His Highness, therefore, repeatedly expressed his concern and solicitude for the condition of his people, and enjoined upon all his officials to distribute relief on a liberal scale. Thirty doctors in addition to the Maharaja's medical staff were engaged from British India, free medical aid was ordered to be supplied far and wide, and every possible precaution adopted to prevent the further spread of the dreadful epidemic.

No sooner the first intimation of the scarcity in Cashmere reached Jummu, than the Maharaja sent Pandit Suraj Koul, Rai Bahadur, the Revenue Member of the Council, to Srinagar, to make arrangements for the supply of rice to the starving population. The Pandit managed the business with which he had been entrusted with efficiency and skill. He sent for the grain-dealers who to raise the rates had held in their stock, appealed to their humanity, and gave them to understand that, if they did not content themselves with 'quick sales and small returns,' the Maharaja's Government would undersell them. The traders in grains were thus induced to give up their cupidity, and bring in their stock to the market. Some rules and regulations were also made by which an ample supply of food-grain was guaranteed, the operation of the recently introduced cash assessment was suspended for the season, and the scarcity which had threatened to swell into the proportions of a direful famine was thus successfully met and overcome.

As for the sufferers from fire, who had been rendered perfectly homeless and in many instances reduced to absolute destitution, orders were issued by the Maharaja to grant them timber free of cost for the construction of their houses, and the total value of the timber thus granted amounted to Rs. 75,000, more or less. I shall on this point quote the testimony of an Anglo-Indian paper, published at Lahore, whose proclivities against the Maharaja are well-known, and whose evidence, therefore, cannot be regarded as partial to the Maharaja. It wrote as follows—'The Maharaja of Cashmere has liberally ordered that a free grant of the net value of Rs. 50, calculated at the State rates of 1890 and 1891, be given from the forest depot at Srinagar to all people whose houses have been burnt in the late fires in the city. Mr. McDonell, the Conservator, has been ordered to bring a sufficient quantity of timber in the city from the nearest forests, and to sell to the people *deodar* and *chil* wood in excess of free-gifts, at the rates of 1890 and 1891, provided the wood thus sold be for the *bona fide* purpose of rebuilding the burnt houses. This generosity will be much appreciated by the long suffering people of Srinagar.'*

In July 1892, the Maharaja went from Jummu to Srinagar. Cholera had not yet been stamped out from the Valley, but the Maharaja could not, nevertheless, longer defer his visit to his afflicted people. He had hitherto put it off owing to the repeated importunities of the Resident, but to do so was a sore trial

---

* The *Civil and Military Gazette*, dated the 28th. October 1892.

to him. Each day's report, as it reached him, of the manifold sufferings of his subjects, cost him heavy sighs, and as he regarded them with paternal tenderness, he was naturally impatient to see their condition with his own eyes, to encourage them with his presence, and console them with his personal sympathy in all their distress. No sooner, therefore, he succeeded in extorting the unwilling consent of the Resident than he hastened to Srinagar, where he was received by the people, in spite of the terrible calamities that had befallen them, with every demonstration of joy and loyalty.

On arrival at Srinagar, the Maharaja had his attention engrossed in considering the most pressing matters, connected with the administration of his State and the welfare of his people. He went after a brief interval to Gulmarg, where the Resident was still sojourning, to confer with the latter as to the best means of alleviating the miseries of his subjects. Then shortly returning to Srinagar, he began to discuss and transact matters of serious import. The sufferers from the late epidemic, fire and scarcity naturally demanded his first care. Having afforded them all available relief, as has been already described above, he next turned his attention to the sanitary improvement of Srinagar. A proposal had emanated from a high quarter that an edict should be issued, making it incumbent on all citizens to leave a certain quantity of vacant land around each dwelling house, for purposes of cleanliness and ventilation. The Maharaja saw the difficulty of giving effect to this proposal. He remembered that in great cities like London, Calcutta and Bombay, such a proposal could not be practicable —much less therefore could it be so in Srinagar. He fully appreciated the benefits of cleanliness and free ventilation, however, and arrived at a compromise by ordering that the proposal should be carried out, as far as possible, in respect of new buildings, but as regards old buildings, they should not be meddled with. There can hardly be two opinions regarding the soundness of this decision.

The Maharaja ordered the widening and construction of a central road along the whole length of the city with wide cross lanes, and other sanitary improvements, which when fully executed will not fail to ward off, or at any rate to mitigate the virulence of, such epidemics as occurred last year. One of the most important of these improvements was a plan for the introduction of a system of water-works in Srinagar. The Maharaja was aware of the modern medical opinion that cholera is propagated more through the drinking water than by any other agency. He was, therefore, desirous of providing the citizens with an abundant supply of undefiled water, which abounds in the vicinity of the city. But he was anxious, at the same time, that the Srinagar water-works might not prove a *fiasco* like those at Jummu where, under the auspices of

Col. Nisbet, the resources of the State had been squandered away in laying a set of ricketty pipes, that could not stand the pressure even of the water pumped into them. The Maharaja, therefore, insisted that, in constructing the waterworks at Srinagar, the maximum of efficiency should be secured with the minimum of outlay. About 4 lakhs of rupees were accordingly sanctioned which, it may be hoped, will be expended in such a way as to render the proposed waterworks a real and lasting boon to the people.

But the condition of the peasant population, for whom the Maharaja has, from the day of his ascending his father's throne, ever felt the most anxious solicitude and interest, was at this time uppermost in his mind. The recent scarcity had brought misery to the door of the masses, and, though with strenuous exertions His Highness had succeeded in giving them relief, their helplessness had made a deep impression upon his mind, and he resolved to bestow on them a permanent and substantial concession. He was aware of the canker of official oppression that was eating into their vitals, and when he had tried to remove that oppression in the first year of his reign, he was not allowed freedom of action. However, now that a fresh opportunity had occurred, he determined to avail of it and to remove, by one stroke of the pen as it were, one of the standing grievances of the people. A large arrear of revenue, aggregating about 37 lakhs of rupees, had been owing by the cultivators since a long time, and the amount was being carried against them in the State accounts from year to year. This arrear had become a continual bugbear, and a source of perennial oppression in the hands of unscrupulous village officials. The Maharaja duly apprehended the evils that resulted in consequence, and he hit upon the resolution of remitting the whole amount of this arrear as the best means of knocking the oppression on the head.

Accordingly, in the grand Durbar, held on the occasion of the Dusserah festival on 30th September 1892, the cultivators of Cashmere—the Moslem cultivators of Sir John Gorst—were in public assembly informed that their ruler had, with royal munificence, forgiven them the payment of this large sum. The Durbar was graphically described by a correspondent of the same Anglo-Indian paper that I have already had occasion to refer to once, and as the picture drawn by him cannot be suspected of exaggeration in favour of the Maharaja, I cannot resist the temptation of giving a few lengthy extracts from his letter.*

Writing on the 4th October 1892, the correspondent said—'The Dusserah festival of 1892 will not be readily forgotton by the people of the Vale of Cashmere, or by any one whose good fortune it was to be present at the great Durbar, held by His Highness Pratap Singh, Maharaja of Jummu and Cashmere, at the Lalmandi

*The *Civil and Military Gazette*, dated 17th October 1892.

Palace, on the 30th September. I have already telegraphed the leading fact that the Maharaja, in a spirit of enlightened and generous statesmanship, announced on this occasion that he had decided to remit arrears of revenue, due from the eleven tehsils which have been brought under the new settlement and assessment, amounting to close upon 35 lakhs of rupees. The shortened limits of a telegraphic message do not allow the correspondent to express the deep impression which such a ceremony as that witnessed on Saturday last made on the on-looker. Seated in open Durbar, surrounded by his brothers and the chief officials of his State, the Maharaja, for the first time since he succeeded to the rule of the fairest provinces of the Indian Empire, looked down on the assembled thousands of the village elders of Cashmere.* The whole court of

---

*The correspondent evidently did not witness the imposing spectacle in the Lalmandi Palace, on the occasion of the Maharaja's first visit to Cashmere after ascending the *guddee*, in August 1886. The scene on that occasion was even more splendid and impressive.

the Lalmandi Palace presented one solid mass of life, the villagers, putting aside for once the dull and ungraceful grey woollen robe which marks the Cashmeri, had clothed themselves in holiday dresses of pure white, and the effect in the brilliant sunlight of an Autumn day was effective in the extreme. Below the surface of the natural dignity and decorum which sets its stamp on a great eastern crowd, seethed and worked the controlled excitement of the masses, brought once more, after many years of estrangement from or rather of absence of personal contact with their Chief, face to face in open assembly with their Ruler. One of the most serious drawbacks attendant on the highly artificial character of our rule in India is, perhaps, the tendency of all bureaucracies to underrate the importance of the strong feeling of loyalty and affection to the person of the ruler. No one acquainted with Jummu and Cashmere can have failed to be impressed with the fact that the ruling family and the Maharaja, and especially the latter, for the villagers cannot grasp the idea of an impersonal rule, centred in a thing called a Council, are regarded with feelings of strong attachment. The Government may have been bad, petty officials may have plundered, the cultivator may have been ground down to the last degree, but his feeling always has been that the Maharaja does not know of the villanies perpetrated in his name, and that from his clemency and honest desire for the welfare of his people, if only he could be reached, would flow kindness, consideration and justice.

'Never was this fact more clearly shewn than on Saturday last. The Maharaja's reception, when he entered the Durbar, was one of which any ruler might be proud. The great crowd was evidently moved as one man with a feeling of respectful and even affectionate gratitude; once again the people felt that their ruler was before them, greeting them in person, the visible embodiment of personal rule.

'The Maharaja's speech, the full

purport of which had not been permitted to leak out, so that its effect was the more impressive, was short, straightforward, decided and most effective. Speaking plainly and distinctly, His Highness addressed the assembly nearly in these terms.' The correspondent then gave a report of the Maharaja's speech which deserves the most attentive perusal, as it lays bare the recesses of His Highness's heart and shews him as a ruler in his true colours.

The Maharaja said—'All of you here present may have heard of my object in convening this meeting. For a long time past, I have cherished in my heart a desire to acquaint my subjects, Muqquddams, Lambardars and gentry, with the measures which have engaged my attention to ensure their welfare and happiness. It is not unknown to you that remissions of arrears, amounting to 24 lakhs of rupees, were made by His Highness the late Maharaja, and that on my accession to the *guddee* a further remission, amounting to some four lakhs of revenue per annum, was made by me. I now take a further opportunity of shewing my special favour by making an announcement marking my anxiety for your welfare. A system of regular settlement has been introduced at considerable expense in Cashmere, with a view to regulate the collection of revenue, and to remove the difficulties experienced by the people in consequence of the absence of fixed assessments; and it is a matter of great pleasure to me that you are satisfied with the settlement and that you have already begun to derive from it the advantage it was intended to confer. Arrears of revenue have been accumulating against you since the year 1879, and you are well aware of the fact that you have been called upon every year to pay some portion of these arrears.

'It is, however, my heart-felt desire to disburden you from these arrears of revenue, so that, freed from the debts which hampered you, the payment of the government revenue which has been moderately assessed may be facilitated for you, cultivation may be increased, lands may be improved, sericulture may again be a flourishing industry, the cultivation of fruits may be taken in hand, and you may return to your fields animated with a feeling of security, of zeal and perseverence.

'I consider it desirable on this occasion to assure you of the fixity of the new assessments during the term for which they have been settled, and to promise you that no alteration whatever shall be made in them during that term, and that you shall continue in the enjoyment of the rights which have been granted to you, provided however that the revenue is punctually paid, and that you continue to maintain your loyalty and allegiance to your Chief.

'It is my hearty wish that my country may daily gain in peace and prosperity and that justice may be done to the people.'

The above speaks for itself. A misconception seems to prevail in certain quarters that the Maharaja's desire for a settlement and reasonable assessment of the land in his territories followed the commencement of settlement operations under the initiation of the British Government. The fact, however, is that, ever since his accession, he had been anxious for a proper settlement, and that was the reason why, in the very first year of his reign, he had applied to Sir Charles Aitchison, then Lieutenant Governor of the Punjab, for the loan of a competent Settlement Officer. It was subsequently decided by the Government of India, however, on the recommendation of Mr. Plowden, then Resident in Cashmere, that Mr. Wingate, who had satisfactorily conducted settlement work in some Native States, should be appointed for the purpose. Mr. Wingate's services were accordingly engaged, and in his report of settlement operations, dated the 1st August 1888, he paid a just tribute to the Maharaja's kingly solicitude for the welfare of his subjects. In para 71 of that report, Mr. Wingate makes the following observations which cannot be too carefully borne in mind—'My account of what is in progress under Your Highness's authority but against Your Highness's interests has been long, because I stand alone, and my mere assertion that the state treasury was being depleted, and the poor were being turned out of their lands, and the staple food of the people had become a monopoly of the officials, would not be believed. I appeal to Your Highness with some confidence, because I have been impressed during my interviews with the belief that Your Highness has a ready sympathy for the poor, a keen interest in land questions, and a determination to protect the cultivators against the officials. But my heart fails me when I think there is no one among those who surround your Highness from whom I can hope for a word in support of my prayer, that one and all will use every argument to pursuade Your Highness that my proposals will be detrimental to the traditions, the policy, or the dignity of the State; that they are impossible, and that neither the rice nor the land should be trusted out of official custody.'

The above renders it as clear as it is possible for language to do that the Maharaja, as I have always contended, has been ever anxious to promote all measures calculated to further the welfare of his subjects, and that if such measures have met with any opposition, the opposition has proceeded not from His Highness, but from those officials of his who have been more favoured and trusted than His Highness himself. The passage quoted proves two things, namely, (1) that the Maharaja has always been in favour of settlement operations, the idea of undertaking them having in fact originated with him; and (2) that it was not the Maharaja but his officials that were responsible for the hardships caused by the delay in carrying out the settlement proposals of Mr. Wingate, though when the settlement was completed these very officials got all the credit but the Maharaja none.

A few days after the Dusserah Durbar described above, an interesting ceremony was performed, which possessed a remarkable significance in the eyes of the people of Cashmere. This was the investiture of the Maharaja with the insignia of the Knight Grand Commandership of the Exalted Order of the Star of India. The ceremony was performed by Col. Prideaux in the Durbar Hall at Srinagar, on 6th October 1892, with an *eclat* befitting the occasion. Two regiments of the Maharaja's forces were drawn up in splendid array in the compound of the palace ; the Maharaja and the Resident, on golden chairs, with His Highness's brothers and all the chief officials and principal *reises* of the State, were seated in barbaric grandeur ; the band played the national Anthem ; and the royal warrant and the statutes conferring the title were read amidst salvos of artillery, proclaiming from the top of Hari Parbut to the citizens and the villagers, far and near, that their beloved Ruler had been honoured with a fitting recognition by the Empress of India. The hearts of the whole population were filled with gladness and joy. The Resident, in a congratulatory speech, complimented the Maharaja on the good management of State affairs; specially alluded to His Highness's liberality in having remitted large outstanding balances of revenue due by the cultivators, who were thereby rescued from much harassment and oppression; dwelt upon various acts of His Highness, shewing his devotion and loyalty to the Paramount Power; and expressed great satisfaction at having been able to perform the ceremony of investiture before going home on furlough. A suitable reply was given by the Maharaja, but the most notable part of the whole programme was that with which the ceremony was wound up, namely, the reading of an address to the Maharaja, which gave expression to the feelings of His Highness's subjects on the auspicious occasion.

This address, after expressing a deep sense of gratitude and thankfulness to the Queen-Empress 'for the kind steps taken last year towards the restoration of our most beloved and kind Maharaja who is the supporter of his dependent subjects,' proceeded as follows—'Our Maharaja is fully alive to the responsibilities of the situation in which he is placed, and is conducting the administration with the utmost tact, ability and energy, and has conferred manifold blessings upon the State and its subjects. His heart is full of devoted loyalty to the Paramount Power, and his sole object is to look to the welfare of the State with due deference to the prestige of the Government of India. Order and good government has been established, considerable progress has been made in the direction of reform, much useful work has been done with regard to almost every branch of the administration. It will be needless to enumerate the good work that has been done by the Maharaja; several good roads have been constructed and widened, much improvement has been effected in the public works, and careful measures have been taken to prevent the scarcity of corn. The cultivators of the soil have been exempted from the payment of about 40 lakhs of rupees, due on account of arrears of revenue. His Highness the Maharaja Saheb has bestowed his careful attention to the settlement operations, and has been greatly pleased to find the operations have been carried on well. Municipal improvements have been effected in the cities of Jummu and Cashmere, much progress has been made in English education in the high schools at Jummu and Cashmere. Many other improvements have been effected which need not be detailed here. Suffice it to say that strict justice is being administered to the public, constant efforts have been made to secure peace and prosperity in the land.

'His Highness the Maharaja Saheb is sparing no pains towards the improvement of the State in every possible way. May he continue to do the good work he has taken in hand, and may God grant him the power and strength to effect these arduous works, and may Her Majesty the Queen Empress continue to shew our Maharaja such marks of her approval of the manner in which he is performing his duties, and to look upon him always as a most faithful ally, and may the Maharaja continue to thrive under the auspices of her Majesty the Queen-Empress.'

Making every allowance for the language of the above address, it is of immense value as being a spontaneous testimony on the part of the Maharaja's subjects, which speaks volumes in his favour. These subjects, Hindus as well as Mahomedans, are fully conscious of the paternal interest which the Maharaja feels in their advancement and welfare, and are in turn animated by filial sentiments towards him. Much has been said of the Maharaja's misgovernment, but ask the people from one end of his territories to the other and they will relate a different tale. They will all agree in extolling his benevolence, his largeheartedness and his kingly qualities. The restoration of the Maharaja, therefore, had naturally sent through them a thrill of joy and exultation, and the bestowal of this mark of special honour—the highest that is conferred on the Princes of the country—stirred up in their breasts those profound emotions which they tried to express in their imperfect utterances in the above address. Misgovernment has existed in Cashmere as a remnant of the misrule and oppression that once prevailed, but the Maharaja is as little responsible for it as the man in the moon. The Maharaja's opponents, on the contrary,—those who have intrigued against him and opposed and thwarted all his beneficial schemes of enlightened administration—are solely responsible for it. And yet, by an irony of fate, these very opponents have obtained credit for all good measures introduced into the State, while he himself has been discredited, degraded and dishonoured. The Maharaja's personal misgovernment is a fiction and a myth, and Lord Lansdowne is to be heartily congratulated on having done the good but unfortunate Prince partial reparation, as already stated. It has been and shall be my duty to prove that His Lordship owes it to himself to render him more complete reparation before leaving this country.

The Maharaja left the Cashmere Valley about the middle of October 1892, and returned to Jummu. Soon after his return to his ancestral home, he devoted his attention among other things, to performing a very interesting duty, namely, giving a suitable valedictory reception and entertainment to His Excellency Lord Roberts, late Commander-in-Chief of Her Majesty's forces in India. The way in which this reception and entertainment were conceived and executed reflected credit on the Maharaja's heart, though the affair must have cost a large sum of money to an exhausted treasury. Such lavish expenditure for such a purpose might be objected to on economical grounds, but the Maharaja had a plausible argument in his favour. He had just returned from Cashmere, somewhat flushed with the turn events had recently taken in his affairs, and he felt that he had special reason to display his gratitude to the only big official in the country who had stood by him through foul and fair. Moreover, for Lord Roberts, who had been his grand-father's and fathers friend, the Maharaja felt a respectful regard, and he spoke truly and sincerely when, in welcoming Lord and Lady Roberts to Jummu, he said—'Your Lordship was one of my late lamented father's good and generous friends, and I have had experience of Your Excellency's kindness from very tender years, and have, moreover, had material help and advice from your Excellency since my accession to the *guddee.* It would not be wrong, therefore, if I said that there were not many in India whose feelings of respect and attachment for Your Excellency surpassed mine. I have always found in Your Excellency a true well-wisher and guide, and now contemplate with deep regret your approaching departure from this country.'

Lord Roberts made a fitting response—'I can assure His Highness that there is no period of my life in India, to which I shall look back, in years to come, with more unalloyed pleasure than the visits I have paid to Cashmere, when, as on the present occasion, I have enjoyed the generous hospitality of the Maharaja of Cashmere, which is a tradition among all Englishmen who have been fortunate enough to visit the Happy Valley. Thirty eight years have passed since I first saw the beautiful Valley of Cashmere, and had the honour of making the acquaintance of His Highness's grandfather, Maharaja Golab Singh. Later, I had the privilege to know His Highness's father, Sir Runbir Singh, and now, as I am about to leave India, I find myself the honoured guest and valued friend of Colonel His Highness Maharaja Sir Pratap Singh.' The Maharaja may well be excused if, with a record of friendship extending over three generations and a keen sense of kindnesses received, he sacrificed a little economy for the sake of friendly and grateful hospitality.

An account of the Maharaja's princely hospitality on this occasion might fill up pages, but such an account would be out of place in a book like this. There are one or two facts, however, which I should not omit to mention at this place. One is the high compliment paid by Lord Roberts to the loyalty and services of the Maharaja. After referring to the improvements effected in the administration, His Excellency observed—'I feel sure that every British officer who takes an interest in the Indian army will, in common with myself, have heard with admiration of the behaviour of the Cashmere troops when, side by side with their comrades of the Regular Army, they gallantly stormed the enemy's position at Nilt in December last, till then thought impregnable by the tribesmen of Hunza-Nagar. As Commander-in-Chief in India, I thoroughly appreciate how materially the force available for the defence of this great Empire has been strengthened by the addition to it of the Imperial Service troops, and I beg His Highness to accept my best thanks for the troops of this State, the services of which have been placed by the Maharaja more than once at the disposal of the government of India, in that spirit of loyalty which has ever been the characteristic of the rulers of Cashmere.' No State, in subordinate alliance with the Government of India, has ever had so many and varied opportunities for the display of its devotion and loyalty and rendering such conspicuous services as Cashmere, yet it is strange to say that the chief of that State should have been, under the *regime* of a noble-minded statesman, accorded a treatment which might be considered unworthy even of those of lukewarm or doubtful allegiance.

Another fact which Lord Robert's visit to Jummu brought to the fore-front was the Maharaja's capacity for sustained work. Making every allowance for the unusual excitement of the occasion, one might say that, it did not show 'imbecility,' which had been attributed to the Maharaja, to be up with the dawn, be on horseback for six hours at a stretch, work in the office during the fixed hours, superintend the details of every preparation, preside at important ceremonies, and retire unexhausted at midnight. Lord Roberts and his companions were eye-witnesses of the Maharaja's energy and business capacity. It is not necessary, therefore, for me to be an apologist for the Maharaja; yet, I may venture to claim it for him that imbecility is not a trait in his character. That he should have been charged with it shews either that the Maharaja's opponents have not been well-informed, or that they have not been very scrupulous about telling the truth.

The farewell entertainment to Lord Roberts took place at Jummu in the beginning of November, 1892. A couple of months later, that is, in the beginning of January 1893, a similar entertainment was given to Lord Roberts by the citizens of Lahore, at which the Maharaja took a prominent part. He was requested to preside over the committee appointed to carry out the details of that entertainment, and he gladly accepted the presidentship. It may appear objectionable, at first sight, that the Maharaja of Cashmere should have come to Lahore, leaving the cares of his State, for the purpose of officiating at such a petty function. But His Highness was not unaware of the criticism to which he was exposing himself. His objects, however, were three-fold: first, Lord Roberts was for the last time visiting the Punjab, and his feeling heart longed to do honour to the one man—a big official to boot—who had spoken to him kind words of encouragement and hope, and promised him help, even in his dire adversity. I have already adverted to the fact that, as stated by Lord Roberts himself in his speech at Jummu, he was the friend of the Maharaja's father and grandfather, that his friendship with the Jummu family had thus extended over three generations, and that he had always shewn his willingness to befriend the Maharaja. An expression of gratitude to such a kind old friend was, therefore, the Maharaja's first object. His next object was to give Lord Roberts one more instance of his warmth of heart and active personal habits, so that His Lordship might carry with him to England pleasant reminiscences of the Maharaja's friendship, and interest himself more zealously in the Maharaja's advancement and prosperity. The last object of the Maharaja was to lay hold of an opportunity to come in contact with progressive methods and ideas, which cannot fail to exercise a beneficent effect over the minds of Indian rulers and chiefs. Isolation is responsible for much of the backwardness in Native States, and the Maharaja is aware that, the more it can be broken through, the more is he likely to benefit himself and his people.

I cannot conclude this part of my subject without paying a compliment to the Maharaja, which every one at Lahore felt it to be His Highness's due on this occasion. His Highness kept himself well in evidence during his brief stay in the capital of the Punjab, mixing rather freely with the *elite* of the Lahore community; and he impressed them all with his urbanity, his frank and genial manners, and his courteous, polite and graceful demeanour. The false notions regarding him that had obtained currency were dispelled, and even Europeans began to think more kindly and charitably of him than they had been accustomed to do.

PART III.

IT is superfluous to observe that the reverses that had come upon Maharaja Pratap Singh in the beginning of 1889 were not of his own seeking. They were the outcome of a combination of circumstances over which he could exercise no control. He was made to suffer for the faults of a system which dated from a period long antecedent to his birth, and which he, on his accession to the *guddee,* had tried his best to modify and improve. His failure to accomplish the desired end was due entirely to the thwarting opposition which had, from the very commencement, dogged him at almost every step. I have already attempted to describe how the immediate predecessors of Col. Prideaux dealt with the Maharaja. The attitude of Mr. Plowden to the Maharaja is rendered clear by the terms in which he spoke of His

Highness in a report to the Government of India, dated the 5th March 1888. After premising that he was 'not actuated by any feelings of personal dislike towards His Highness', the Resident proceeded—'I think, however, the Government of India should be under no illusion as regards Maharaja Pratap Singh. From first to last, I have failed to discover in him any sustained capacity for governing his country, or any genuine desire to ameliorate its condition, or to introduce those reforms which he has acknowledged to be necessary. More than two years have passed since his accession, but not only has he achieved nothing, but he has opposed beneficial measures proposed by others.'

The Resident continued in this strain, not knowing or forgetting everything about the multiplicity of reforms introduced by the Maharaja in the first year of his rule—reforms clean swept away by his own favourite and protege

Dewan Luchman Das; and 'most earnestly advised the Government of India that the Maharaja be made plainly to understand that he has had his chance and that he will not be allowed any longer to stand in the way.' He wound up by suggesting that the Maharaja should be assigned a liberal income but excluded from all real power. 'I consider,' he added, 'that a reduction of the Maharaja's authority on these lines is an essential condition precedent to all other necessary measures.' He then proposed three alternative schemes for the administration of the Maharaja's territories, in none of which did he give the Maharaja himself any place.*

The Resident submitted the above report to the Government of India along with the Maharaja's *kharita*, dated the 13th April 1888, in which the Maharaja had proposed his own plan of administration, having had no notice of the mischief that was

* Cashmere Bluebook pp. 17-18

brewing against him. Thus a strenuous attempt was made to injure the unfortunate Prince behind his back. Lest the Government of India should suspect anything wrong in such extreme proposals of the Resident, the latter had the foresight to premise, as already stated, that he was not actuated by any personal feelings against the Maharaja. But Lord Dufferin had the penetration to see beneath the surface of things, and the good sense to reject the Resident's relentless proposals. The Secretary to the Government of India, in his letter dated the 25th July 1888, wrote to the Resident informing him that 'the Government of India has decided to accept in principle the scheme which His Highness has put forward, and your own alternative proposals have for the present been set aside.' The Secretary, after conveying certain general instructions, concluded his letter in these words—'The Governor General in Council does not consider it necessary to give you more detailed instructions with regard to the course which you should pursue. He has no doubt that a consideration of this letter and of the enclosed *kharita* will suffice to show the principles upon which he desires you to act, and he hopes that, with the aid of judicious and sympathetic advice on your part, the Maharaja may, before you leave Cashmere, have succeeded at least in laying the foundations of an efficient scheme of Government.'* It would have been productive of the happiest results if Mr. Plowden had been able to afford the Maharaja his judicious and sympathetic advice, and thus realise the hope entertained by Lord Dufferin. Far from giving the Maharaja such advice, however, the Resident treated His Highness with so much superciliousness that Lord Dufferin felt himself called upon to remove him from the Cashmere Residency, as has been mentioned before.

It would be superfluous now to contra-

* Parliamentary Bluebook pp. 20-21.

dict categorically the statement made by Mr. Plowden in his above report with regard to the Maharaja. It will have been satisfactorily found out ere this that, far from obstructing reforms, the Maharaja has been only too anxious and forward to advance them by every means in his power. Mr. Plowden's estimate of the Maharaja was, therefore, entirely erroneous; and it may be interesting to note his remarks in the same report, regarding Raja Sir Amar Singh, in connection with the proposal to appoint the latter to the Cashmere Premiership. He said—'I have great doubts whether Raja Amar Singh can be trusted, and unless he has a strong officer at his elbow to keep him straight, I do not think it would be safe to employ him. He has never forgotten his father's intentions on his behalf, and the object he is working for is to become Maharaja of Cashmere. Once he gets power into his own hands, he will use it without scruple to attain this end.' It is difficult to reconcile this display of sagacity in the one instance with the purblindness manifested in the other.

Writing on a previous occasion, I dwelt at some length upon the reforms initiated by Maharaja Pratap Singh during the first year of his reign and the difficulties which led to their failure. I summed up these reforms under five heads, namely, administrative, fiscal, economical, judicial and educational, and described them in some detail.* These reforms had not only been planned out on paper, but some of them, particularly those regarding the reduction or abolition of obnoxious imposts or duties, along with some other beneficial ones, had actually been carried out in practice. The rest, however, did not enure because, as justly remarked by Lord Lansdowne in his speech at Srinagar on 24th October 1891,—'the real difficulties of reformation begin when reforms, which have been elaborated on paper, come to be submitted to the test of practical application.' In the Maharaja's case,

* My 'Cashmere and its Prince,' pp. 11—22.

these difficulties were greatly enhanced owing principally to two causes, that is, first, the thick phalanx of opposition, which the Maharaja met with from an influential though hopelessly corrupt body of officials, who flourished by the existence of abuses in the administration; and secondly, the total absence of sympathetic help on the part of the Resident who, though bound to give him every encouragement and support, did his best practically to foil him in every possible way.

It would be unnecessary to burden those pages with a detail of the above reforms, which I dwelt upon in 1889. I should rather try to give here briefly some idea of the good work done by the Maharaja, or at his instance, since his restoration in November 1891. I have already referred to the Maharaja's interest in the land settlement, to his anxiety for the welfare of his peasantry, and to the generous remission of arrears of revenue granted by him at the Dusserah Durbar last year.

I have also mentioned the measures ordered by him for granting on a liberal scale medical relief, pecuniary help and other assistance to the sufferers from a fell epidemic, disastrous fires and dire scarcity. The fixity of the land tenure, followed by the generous remission of arrears of revenue, has given an impetus to the breaking up of the waste land which has been reclaimed in large quantities since last year.

The accounts of the State had lapsed into such hopeless confusion that it had been found necessary, about the middle of 1891, to depute Mr. Logan from Lahore, for the purpose of making a full enquiry into their condition. The supreme importance of introducing a sound system of audit and account, which Lord Lansdowne justly said was 'the very back-bone and essence of good administration, whether in a Native State or in an Indian Province', was well-known to the Maharaja, who as early as 1886 had conceived the idea of engaging the services of an experienced Indian officer for placing the State accounts in proper order—an idea which could not be then carried out owing to circumstances which shortly overtook His Highness. No sooner, therefore, was the appointment of Mr. Kiernander to the Accountant Generalship of Cashmere proposed, than the proposal was readily agreed to by His Highness. With a proper system of accounts, greater economy and more land brought under cultivation, the revenue has since slightly gone up, while the expenditure has shewn a tendency towards decrease. The budget estimate for the current year shews a deficit of only about seven lackhs of rupees, while last year the deficit amounted to about eighteen lackhs. The Governorships of both Jummu and Cashmere have, as a prelude to enforcing greater official integrity, changed hands, some notorious intriguers have been ordered out of the State, and attempts have been made to purify the judicial administration and place the executive on a sounder or more effective basis. The Criminal Code has been amended, the laws of limitation and evidence have been enacted, and several useful judicial circulars issued ; while certain Chiefs have been invested with the powers of Honorary Magistrates within defined jurisdictions.

The Maharaja has given his cordial assent to the proposal for the reclamation of waste land near Bunji and Gilgit. Mr. Lawrence, Settlement Officer, made in consequence a tour of inspection in June last. The Road to Gilgit has been pushed on ; the Indus bridge, called after His Highness, the Pratap Bridge, and the Ramghat Bridge have been completed; and the section of the Jhelum Valley Road from Baramula to Srinagar is shortly going to be taken in hand. The sanitation and conservancy of Srinagar have been improved by the widening and construction of the central road and the cross-lanes, and providing public latrines in every part of the city. The Srinagar water-works have been sanctioned, and nearly

4 lakhs of rupees allotted for the same. The bridge across the Tavi has been finished and opened for public traffic. The Jummu School has been proposed to be raised to the status of a college, and a similar proposal is under consideration with regard to the School at Srinagar. The *begar* cess which used to be levied from the zemindars has been remitted, and the wages of coolies raised to 4 annas per head per day, a rate which would be considered respectable even in British India; and as an effective check on forced labour, private agency has been engaged on the Jhelum Valley as well as the Banehal Road, for the supply of coolies and horses on hire.

The Mian Rajputs, descended from the same stock as the Maharaja, who were hard up for their livelihood, have been granted land under the settlement regulations, and this important community has thereby been put in the possession of means for earning their bread. The army organisation has gone on improving, and about Rs. 180,000, arrears due in the Military Department against Sepoys, have been remitted. The farm of the Customs duties has been leased out for three years at an increased profit of Rs. 40,000 per year, while, to stimulate trade in Jummu, orders have been issued by His Highness in every department to make purchases of all State supplies and stores through the dealers in the city. Vigorous steps have been adopted to prevent the recurrence of small-pox in Ladakh. Raja Buldeo Singh has been installed on the throne of Punch under a new treaty, sunnuds have been granted to the chiefs of Hanza and Nagar, while the relations of the Maharaja with his feudatories have been put on an improved and more satisfactory footing. The Mission Hospital has been supported and helped, the Mastgurh Musjid, which had been shut up for generations, has been thrown open to the Mahomedans, and perfect freedom of religious discussion and practice tolerated and allowed. The Maharaja, a patron of letters by inclination and by the very virtue of his dignity, has not forgotten the encouragement of the classical literature of his country. He has given every facility to Dr. Stein of the Punjab University for the publication of the *Raja-Tarangini*, or the history of Cashmere in Sanskrit, given a donation of Rs. 500 to the translator of the *Charaka-Sanhita*, an ancient Sanskrit medical work, and,more recently, another donation of Rs. 1000 to the well-known translator of the Mahabharata to enable him to complete his gigantic task.

The above list of works, accomplished within the brief period of a year and a half, cannot be treated as light. The list is not exhaustive, but it consists of many of the principal items, and should be considered satisfactory even by the fault-finding or the fastidious. It shews as clearly as anything that the Maharaja has made good use of his time since his restoration. The first half of this time was much occupied in conciliating or overcoming opposition. It is only latterly that he has been able to devote his undivided attention to the affairs of his State, and considering all things, one may be prepared to concede that he has succeeded marvellously well.

It would have afforded me unmixed satisfaction to notice at this place that the Maharaja's brothers were now on perfectly dutiful terms with His Highness. His second brother Raja Ram Singh was at one time his zealous supporter, but intriguers had some time ago prevailed upon the latter and caused him to defect from the Maharaja. Both he as well as Raja Sir Amar Singh have, however, since, outwardly at least, returned to their allegiance, and they deserve congratulation if they have sincerely done so. According to the injunctions of the Hindu scriptures, the elder brother should be looked upon as the father, and the great Bard of ancient India has exhausted all the vigour and resources of his sublime genius in preaching, among other duties, the claims of fraternal good-will, affection and respect. When Rama Chandra became exiled to the great forests of Dandaka, Lakshmana would not stay at home but must follow his eldest brother, sharing with him all his dangers, his joys and his sorrows. And when Bharata, who had been sojourning at his maternal uncle's, returned to Ayodhya and found that his father had died and Rama Chandra had left for the wilderness, he became disconsolate, turned a deaf ear to his mother's importunities to place the diadem on his own head, and hurried forth in search of his exiled brothers. He traced them out in their wild retreat, wept bitterly for all that had taken place, and earnestly and passionately besought them to return to the sweets of kingdom and home. But the truthful son of Dasaratha, who never recanted a spoken word, informed him that he could not change his purpose, but must serve out his term of banishment, and insisted upon Bharata returning to Ayodhya and governing the country in his absence. What did the latter then do ? He returned home in obedience to his elder's order it is true, but instead of wearing the crown himself, he placed Rama Chandra's sandals on the throne, elevated the royal umbrella over them, and taking his seat at the foot of the throne, ruled the kingdom as Rama Chandra's minister and lieutenant till his return !

The Ramayana is one of the sacred books of the Hindus. It regulates the conduct, guides the actions and moves the smiles and tears of upwards of two hundred millions of human beings. It teaches one-sixth of the human race lessons of filial reverence and duty, of fraternal affection, of conjugal devotion, of self-sacrifice, fidility and truthfulness such as no other book in the world can. And the lessons of such a book should not be lost upon the people inhabiting this country, and least of all upon royal brothers, tracing their descent to an ancient line of kings, who should in all essentials conform to the sacred traditions of the country, and establish by their conduct their claims to the respect and deference which are their due by reason of their birth.

It is not only as a duty, however, but also as a matter of self-interest that they should be thoroughly loyal and obedient to their eldest brother and chief. They must have fully perceived ere this that the late dissensions among themselves have ended in much loss to the State and their family, but done little good to themselves. One of them, for instance, has been used only as a catspaw by a designing and ambitious autocrat, whose removal from Cashmere has been a blessing to both Prince and people. Raja Sir Amar Singh, clever and intelligent as he is, must have fully perceived before this the wreck he has been instrumental in causing to his own house. He must have also seen that the more he allows himself to play into the hands of ostensible friends but disguised enemies, the less he will advance his own *real* interests and the severer will be the shock to the dynasty of Maharaja Golab Singh. The matter is so clear and legible that one who runs may read, and the wonder is that a quick-witted Prince like him should have ever failed to notice it.

But bye-gones are bye-gones and should be buried in oblivion. Let the brothers henceforth stand arm to arm and support the Maharaja, behave towards him with greater sincerity, and act with him in mutual harmony and co-operation in all matters, public or private. Let them conduct themselves with greater reason and prudence in future, remember that a house divided against itself cannot stand, and bear in mind the duties they owe to themselves, their State and their country; let them not lose sight of the fact that the whole of India has her eyes turned towards them to see how they acquit themselves in their eminent and responsible positions; let them realize that the people of Arya Varta are ready to accede to them the privilege of leadership if they can only rise up, morally and intellectually, to the dignity of their rank and station; let them understand that they have a grander and more important mission to perform than accumulating riches, winning authority or wallowing in sensual enjoyments; let them conceive that they should rather entitle themselves to a country's gratitude and benediction than its contempt and ridicule: and they will experience no difficulty in seeking out the straight path of rectitude and in walking manfully along it, irrespective of the petty considerations of ignoble pelf and short-lived power, or the mischievous delusions caused by time-serving hypocrisy and unscrupulous flattery.

I have touched briefly upon the character of Maharaja Pratap Singh as a ruler, and tried to impart an idea of the beneficent work performed by him during the last eighteen months. One of the latest incidents in his career was the Durbar held at Jummu on 10th March last, for the distribution of medals granted by Her Majesty the Queen Empress to the soldiers of His Highness's army, who had distinguished themselves in the Black Mountain expedition of 1888. The speech made by the Maharaja on this occasion was one that deserves greater attention than has been accorded to it. It shews the depth of His Highness's loyalty to the Paramount Power, and shames those who had brought against him the charge of bad faith and disaffection. Addressing the audience before him, the Maharaja delivered himself as follows—'I cannot let this opportunity pass without giving expression to the feelings which have arisen in me in this Durbar—a Durbar which, to all intents and purposes, is, I believe, to be considered as a purely military assemblage. It is gratifying to me to think that, although my ancesters have, on various occasions, given substantial and manifest proof of their allegiance and loyalty to the Paramount Power, I have also had the good fortune of evincing my devotion to the throne, by rendering some services, however slight they were, in the Black Mountain expedition of 1888.......The offer of troops which I made on the occasion was kindly accepted by the Government of India, and right glad and honoured was I the day when one thousand men of my army marched towards Sialkote for Hazara to take part in that expedition. Similar offers made by me during the last two Black Mountain expeditions received due acknowledgment from the Government of India.

'The services rendered by the men in 1888 have met with the due and kind appreciation of Her Gracious Majesty the Queen Empress of India who, I am glad to say, has been graciously pleased to grant medals for them—medals which coming as a gift from our Sovereign are beyond all price and are invaluable as a mark of Her Majesty's gracious kindness.

'Col. Barr, I request the favour of your

kindly conveying my heart-felt gratitude to His Excellency the Viceroy, who in every way and always takes much kindly interest in promoting the success of all my affairs, for his having moved Her Majesty to grant the medals during his tenure, and of asking His Excellency to convey the same with expressions of my profound respects, loyalty and homage to Her Majesty.

'It is an occasion which begets many a healthy feeling in us. On the one hand, it exhilarates my heart with joyous sentiments and is conducive to the strengthening of the already deeply-rooted feelings of devotion to the Throne, and, on the other, appeals to the heart of every soldier and is a stimulus to him, for the performance of such acts of conspicuous gallantry as might entitle him to similar honours.

'Military officers and soldiers, I must say, before concluding, a word or two of advice to you. Wherever you may be engaged in defending the interests of the

Empire which comprises the interests of this State, you must always make a true display of martial spirit, and try with your body and soul to serve earnestly, loyally and faithfully. Feelings of true manliness must always govern and guide you, as humanity consists in true manliness.'

There is a ring of earnest sincerity in the above which cannot fail to move and convince the most sceptical reader. It is out of the fulness of his heart that the Maharaja speaks, and his words possess a directness of aim and singleness of purpose that cannot be mistaken. The concluding passage would do credit to a crowned head of Europe. One who not only conceives but realises that 'humanity consists in true manliness' is certainly far removed from those aspersions that have been thrown broad-cast upon him. As for the Maharaja's loyalty, it seems to have sought out and filled every nook and corner of his heart and firmly rooted itself there. The Maharaja is loyal by habit, by training and by heredity. In his letter to the Viceroy, dated the 14th May 1889, he wrote to say—'As advised by my late lamented father from my very childhood, my heart is full of loyalty to the Paramount Power, and I am always ready to do all that can be desired by the blessed Government.' And who that knows the history of the life of Maharaja Runbir Sing, will for a moment forget the sentiments of loyalty that inspired him at all moments of his life? The invaluable services that he rendered to the British Government in the dreadful crisis of 1857 are recorded in indelible letters; yet when Sir John Lawrance, after the suppression of the Mutiny, went to Jummu and proposed to reward him for those services, mark the reply of the high-souled Prince—'that he would take no recompense for his share in suppressing the rebellion, but that he would request the Government to remain custodian of the proposed reward for him and let it remain as an item of deposit in the Government exchequer.' Most of the other States that helped the Government in the Mutiny were offered and accepted compensation for services rendered in those terrible days, but Cashmere, while excelling all others in the nature, character and extent of its services, thankfully declined to barter its sense of duty and receive a return for having discharged it.

It would require more space than I can spare to make even a bare mention of all the services that the Jummu family have done to the British Government since the establishment of British authority in the Punjab. The annexation of that province would have been much more difficult but for the help and co-operation of Maharaja Golab Singh. The result of the Sikh wars might, indeed, have assumed a different shape, had he joined the army of the Khalsa and thrown in the weight of his prudence, foresight, influence and prowess on the side of the Durbar at Lahore. The fate of the conflict was for a time almost trembling in the balance, and the situation is thus described by an eminent Ex-Lieutenant Governor of the Punjab—'Taken aback by the determined resistance of the Khalsa troops in the first battles on the banks of the Sutlej, crippled by the loss of a seventh of our army, paralysed by the exhaustion of the artillery ammunition, the want of heavy guns and the deficiency of supplies, which the Cis-Sutlej feudatories began to withhold, the English were reduced to inactivity for a time after the desperate battle of Ferozeshah, and were unable to follow up their victory.'* The fields of Sobraon at such a juncture might have unfolded a different story had not Golab Singh stood aloof from the contest, and, later, the Board of Administration and the Chief Commissioner would not have found it so easy to quell the disturbances that infested the country, except with the help of his prestige and power.

The services of Cashmere in 1857, when Golab Singh had just died and Runbir Singh succeeded him to the throne, have been acknowledged by the historian and in

*Aitchison's Lawrence p. 40.

the records of the Government. A large contingent was sent to co-operate with the British forces at the siege of Delhi. Some suspicion was at first entertained regarding the good faith and the fidelity of this contingent, but the 'Saviour of the Punjab' treated the suspicion as unworthy and wrote to General Wilson in these words —'So far as I have the means of judging, I consider the Jummu troops are trustworthy. I myself would trust them if I were in your place, so long as I had no reason to do otherwise. I think that unless the officers with them are wilfully blind or place stupid confidence in them, they will be able to form a fair, indeed, a just judgment as to their merits, by the time the force gets at Umballa. If by that time my brother has no reason for distrusting them, I would say by all means have them sent on to Delhi and let them aid in the attack.........My own impression is that they will behave well.'* And well was

* Smith's Life of Lawrence Vol. II. p. 184.

the prophecy fulfilled and the suspicion shewn to be entirely groundless, for the Jummu troops bore the brunt of Bukht Khan's attack at the Lahori Gate and took a prominent part in other engagements at the seige of Delhi.

It was not with men nor with money alone, however, that Maharaja Runbir Sing assisted the British Government in those days, but he rendered active service in various other ways. For instance, he seized about 2,000 mutineers that had entered his territories from the side of Hoti Mardan, delivered them to the British authorities, and afforded protection to and treated the English ladies and gentlemen who were in Cashmere with the utmost kindness and hospitality. Lord Canning was so impressed with Maharaja Runbir Singh's invaluable services in such an awful crisis that he wrote a letter to him, assuring him of the gratitude of the British Government and of the benefits that he would be sure to reap by an alliance with it.

A few years after the Mutiny, there

was the Hazara expedition and later on the Yarkand Mission. The doings of Russia in central Asia demanded constant and careful attention. And then within the last few years, the Agror Valley and the Black Mountain expeditions have excited considerable interest both in England and in India. The part played by the Maharaja of Cashmere on all these occasions is well-known and has been publicly acknowledged. The Cashmere forces have more recently subdued the complications in Chitral and Hunza Nagar, made their mark among the Imperial Service Corps that have been formed in the leading Indian States during the last few years, and won their laurels in difficult and arduous campaigns. Cashmere money has, moreover, been freely spent during the last 4 years in strengthening and solidifying the defences of the Empire on the North Western Frontier.

It will have appeared clearly from the foregoing pages that the loyalty of Maharaja Pratab Singh is ardent and devoted, and that the services of his family to the Paramount Power have been varied, continuous and invaluable. The claims of the Maharaja upon the kindness and consideration of the British Government are, therefore, proportionately strong. The compensation that was thankfully declined after the Mutiny by his father, who kept it 'in custody in the British exchequer', has not yet been demanded, but that only imparts additional strength to his claims, and these certainly should be neither forgotten nor over-looked by a Government whose prestige is based even more upon its moral than its material superiority.

Yet it would seem as if those claims have been altogether over-looked and forgotten. The Maharaja was deposed in 1889 on allegations of certain mis-government in Cashmere which, the slightest enquiry would have shown, had been in existence in the State before he or perhaps his father was born. The Maharaja courted an enquiry but it was never granted to him. In a letter addressed by the Government of India to the Secretary of State, dated the 29th July 1889, it was stated against the Maharaja that, under his misrule, the population of the State, in spite of its great natural resources, 'had steadily dwindled and its people had become impoverished to the point of chronic scarcity', and that 'neither his abilities nor his inclinations are likely to bring about any appreciable improvement in the condition of the people committed to his charge.' The Maharaja's deposition was sought to be justified on these statements.

An examination of these statements would, I submit, clearly shew the inadequate and unreliable nature of the information, upon which the Government of India had been moved to take action against the Maharaja. The statements were based principally upon Mr. Wingate's Settlement Report, to which I have already had occasion to refer. It was relied upon as containing 'abundant evidence that most of the abuses continued to prevail unchecked.'*

* Cashmere Bluebook p. 30.

I take up first the question of the decrease of population in Cashmere. Mr. Wingate, in his above report, gives a table of the population of Cashmere proper from 1815 to 1887, and remarks that 'the general result of the last 70 years appears to be that the population is now little more than half of what it used to be. That it is considerably less there can be little doubt.'* He states that the population in 1815 was 800,000, in 1835 it dwindled down to 200,000, in 1873 it rose to 500,000, while in 1887, that is, during the rule of the present Maharaja, it again fell to between 300,000 to 400,000. The margin between the two figures given for 1887 is a wide one, and shews that Mr. Wingate had no reliable statistics to go upon, but was only making a guess. His guess, moreover, was a most haphazard one, and seems to have been a foregone conclusion—more the effect than the cause of his theory of decrease of population in

*Cashmere Bluebook p. 51.

Cashmere in recent years. This can be found at a glance from the last Census Report for the territories which acknowledge the Maharaja's sway. The report was elaborately prepared by Pundit Bhag Ram, Rai Bahadur, the Judicial Member of the Cashmere Council, who had been appointed Census Commissioner for the State at the instance and with the concurrence of the Resident, and whose calculations, considering that he is an old and trusted servant of the British Government, may be regarded as perfectly unimpeachable. This report shews that the population of Cashmere proper on the night of the 28th February 1891, that is, only about three years later, was 949,041, or between two to three times greater than that given by Mr. Wingate !* This figure is eloquent and condemns Mr. Wingate's haphazard guess much more strongly than it is possible for any language to do.

---

* Census Report of the Cashmere State for 1891 p. 14

If the other figures given by Mr. Wingate in his report be at all correct, they would rather point to a different conclusion from that arrived at by him. Those figures would rather tend to shew an increase of population from 1835 when, on account of severe earthquakes followed by cholera in 1824 to 1828 and a severe famine caused by heavy rainfall in 1831 to 1833, it had reached the minimum on record. There were several floods and epidemics between 1835 to 1873. Nevertheless, the population went on rapidly increasing, till it reached the maximum ever known in the reign of Maharaja Pratap Singh. The theory of the decrease of population under the Maharaja's 'misrule,' therefore, entirely falls to the ground.

With regard to the poverty of the people, the statement that they 'had become impoverished to the point of chronic scarcity,' is open to the most serious question. European travellers in Cashmere have often borne testimony to the comparative plenty in which the masses in that State live, as compared with their brethren in many parts of British India. But such testimony may be disregarded as possibly based upon partial observation or in-sufficient data. The result of careful official investigation, conducted under the auspices of the British Resident during the Maharaja's deposition, however, deserves every weight and consideration, and it discloses a state of things far other than that discovered by Mr. Wingate. We read—'There is no ground for the theory advanced by certain critics that the majority of the people are starving. It might be said with certainty about the natives of the State that they are fairly solvent and well to do.' And, again,—'Agriculturists here, comprising 69 per cent of the total population, are remarkably free from debt. The mode of living is very simple, provisions in the interior are cheap, and the people live in peace and harmony'.* The very fact that during the

*The Census Report of the Cashmere State for 1891 p. 117

period ending with 1891, there was an influx of 86,153 persons into Cashmere, of whom 65,108 came from the Punjab and the neighbouring States,* clearly shews that the poverty theory has no legs to stand upon. This influx consisted of 44,481 males and 41,672 females,thus proving that it was not a floating population, but one that had for the most part actually settled with family and children and taken up their abode in the country. People never think of immigrating in large numbers from prosperous localities, such as the Punjab districts may be taken to be, into a place where impoverishment 'to the point of chronic scarcity' is said to prevail.

The charge that the Maharaja had not the inclination to improve the condition of his people can be best refuted by quoting Mr. Wingate himself. In para 71 of his report, from which I have given an extract before,† Mr. Wingate gives the

---

*The Census Report of the Cashmere State for 1891 p. 119.

†See pages 96-97 *ante*.

Maharaja credit for 'a ready sympathy with the poor, a keen interest in land questions, and a determination to protect the cultivators against the officials,' and throws the whole burden of opposition to a fair land settlement on the Maharaja's officials, from the Prime Minister downwards, not one of whom could be hoped to support Mr. Wingate's proposals, but 'one and all' of whom agreed in arguing that those proposals were 'detrimental to the traditions, the policy or the dignity of the State'.* Mr. Wingate joined his appointment as Settlement Officer in Cashmere on 15th January 1887, and wrote his report on 1st August 1888. During the interval between these two dates, the Prime Ministership was occupied not by a Maharaja's selection but by a *protege* of the Resident, who had been thrust upon the Maharaja, and who, under the protection afforded to him by his patron, so thoroughly mismanaged the affairs of the State, as to lead even the *Pioneer* to con-

*Cashmere Bluebook pp. 75-76.

fess that the administration of Cashmere under Dewan Luchman Das was a 'phenomenal failure.' It is robbing Peter to pay Paul to condemn the Maharaja and praise his refractory subordinates in the way it has been the custom to do.

But Mr. Wingate's testimony in favour of the Maharaja is only incidental. More direct testimony of his inclination to better the condition of his subjects is furnished by the history of his reign, the whole of which has been characterized by his deep and earnest anxiety for the happiness and prosperity of his subjects. At the very outset of his career, Sir O. St. John complimented him on the 'valuable boon' he had conferred on his people,* and even a careless study of his subsequent career would amply bear out the favourable impression he then created. Yet, if he has been humbled and punished, that is more his misfortune than his fault.

As for the Maharaja's abilities, I should be loathe to claim for him any extra-

*See pages 29-30 *ante*.

ordinary brilliancy or vigour of intellect. Yet I would stand up for him if he were called incompetent, and maintain that, in all matters connected with the administration, his information is second to no one's in the State. He is possessed of a fund of plain common sense and has got an inquisitive turn of mind, which keep him abreast of the duties and functions he is called upon to perform. But if he is not too clever, he is too kind, generous and sympathetic, and his head and heart together make him as estimable on the whole as most men in the world. It is quite wrong, therefore, to accuse him with want of abilities, especially when it is borne in mind that men in his circumstances do and must depend upon the help of trained intellects in managing their affairs. Crowned heads as a rule are neither great thinkers nor actors; their ministers think and act for them. It is a truism to say that if Maharaja Pratap Singh, with all his generous intincts, had been allowed the services of ministers of his choice, he would have realized the ambition of his life and made Cashmere a 'model' Indian State.

CONCLUSION.

It will have abundantly appeared from the preceding pages that none of of the charges brought against the Maharaja are sustainable, that he is thoroughly loyal to the British Government, that he is an ardent well-wisher of his subjects, that he is not a tyrant but is full of kindness and benevolent intentions, that he always tried his best to improve the administration in all its branches, that his failure has been due to causes beyond his control, that the misgovernment in his State has been very much magnified and exaggerated, and that he has been held responsible for defects in the government of his State which were handed down from generation to generation. The Maharaja, as I have observed before, had fallen a victim to misrepresentations which vanished, like mists before the rising sun, on the appearance of Lord Lansdowne in Cashmere. He had submitted to his reverses with patient dignity and awaited with fortitude the triumph of truth over falsehood. His anticipations have been partly verified. But, under the circumstances mentioned above, he deserves ampler justice than has been meted out to him. His strong claims to the kindness and consideration of the British Government have been already referred to.* It would seem that those claims have not received any attention up to this time. They have been rather neglected and overlooked and ignored.

I am exceedingly sorry to have to record this, but the task I have taken upon myself leaves me no option in the matter. Duty impels me to tell the plain truth, even at the risk of giving offence, though I feel convinced that a love of truth is instinctive with all Englishmen, and no one can fall in their estimation for speak-

* See page 144 *ante*.

ing it. The Maharaja's qualities of head and heart, his family history, the incidents of his own life, his conduct in his adversity, and his career subsequent to his restoration, all cry out loudly in his favour. They all demand that the wrong that has been done to him may be repaired, and he may be once more put in possession of the rights and privileges to which he was born and which he enjoyed on his succession.

It is needless to dilate on those rights and privileges at this place. The treaty of Amritsar, which guaranteed in 1846 to Maharaja Golab Singh and his heirs male the *independent* possession *for ever* of all the dominions secured to him by that treaty, does not require a mention, nor is it necessary to quote again the words of Her Majesty's Proclamation of 1858, which announced to the Princes of India that all treaties and engagements made with them by the East India Company would be scrupulously observed.* The

* See page 21 *ante*.

Paramount Power is fully aware of the status conferred on the Maharaja of Cashmere by the said treaty, and of its obligation to maintain that status in all its integrity. I have shewn before that the Maharaja never did anything to forfeit that status, but it was only on account of a false notion regarding the Maharaja's misgovernment that the status was wrested from him. Now that the mistake has been cleared up, justice as well as sound policy requires that it should be rendered back to His Highness.

And for this I would venture to lay an humble appeal before His Excellency Lord Lansdowne who has, by words as well as by deeds, shewn a willingness to do the Maharaja every reasonable reparation. His Excellency was an unwitting instrument of the Maharaja's downfall, and I trust I have been able to prove clearly that it is due to himself as well as the Maharaja that he should, before leaving India, restore to him those rights and privileges upon which, he publicly declared, the Government of India never harboured for a moment any 'ulterior designs.'* The Maharaja, innocent from the beginning, has served out his probation admirably well, and no ground now remains for keeping him under the ban of displeasure. Col. Nisbet in his letter to the Prime Minister, dated the 17th April 1889, which, by one stroke of the pen, transferred the government of Cashmere from the Maharaja to the hands of the Council, wrote to say that the Viceroy and Governor-General in Council, 'after full consideration of affairs in the Cashmere State for a long time past, has ordered me to inform His Highness the Maharaja that, for a time at least, he will be expected to refrain from all interference in the administration.' Two years and a half elapsed from the date of this letter, and the above order was partly withdrawn, the Maharaja being installed into the Presidentship of his Council. Two years more have since rolled away, but the

---

* See page 67 *ante*.

Maharaja, though he has amply shewn his ability to take charge of his own affairs, is still held in leading strings and kept under the Resident's control.

Lord Cross, from his place in the House of Lords, pledged more than 4 years ago that the Maharaja would be given back all his powers 'no sooner the situation in that quarter is remedied.' I submit the time has arrived for redeeming this pledge of the then Secretary of State. The situation referred to has been more than sufficiently remedied. A number of reforms have been introduced into the State, the settlement operations have made fair progress, large remissions of revenue have been made to relieve the peasant population from the pressure of chronic indebtedness, some obnoxious imposts and duties have been abolished, the frontier defences and communications have been nearly completed, the unruly tribes on the border have been subjugated, the army has reached a high degree of efficiency and rendered valuable active service, roads and works of public utility have been constructed, the accounts, the forests and some other departments of the State have been officered by reliable men, and, on the whole, the machinery of administration has been adjusted in the way desired by the British Government. There are, I submit, no reasons now, for withholding from the Maharaja his just rights and his privileges any longer.

I do not mean to contend that the administration of Cashmere is not capable of such further improvement as may be effected only by properly balanced and duly centralised authority. The system now in force in Cashmere is that of double government which has always proved a failure. There is the Council on the one side with the Maharaja at its head, and there is the Resident on the other; and all measures passed by the Council is subject to the Resident's veto. Though the Resident, therefore, really governs in the name of the Council, the Council is not devoid of responsibility, and has to legislate and administer for itself. The Council again is composed of heterogeneous elements with the Maharaja at its head. But as these elements are independent of him, he naturally finds it difficult to control them, subject as they are to opposing forces and conflicting interests. The difficulty that arises in consequence is considerable, and the only way to obviate it and make the machinery work smoothly is to centralise power in the Maharaja's hands, and constitute him the *de facto* as he is the *de jure* head of the administration. The normal condition of all oriental governments is a benevolent despotism in which all real authority vests in the ruling Prince, and it is impossible that Cashmere should be continued as an independent State and be well governed at the same time, with the system that now prevails in it. The Maharaja burns with a constant desire to regain his good name as a ruler, but he finds himself so hampered on all sides that he nearly despairs of doing so.

Intrigue, in the first place, which is the bane of most administrations in this country, is, it is to be regretted, as predominant in Cashmere at this moment as it used to be before. And the reason is not far to seek. The Maharaja, though the ostensible head of the State, is still powerless to assert himself. His opponents are many and powerful, and they are naturally encouraged in their harmful policy of combining to oppose and thwart him, when they find they can do so with impunity and with advantage to themselves. The Maharaja has throughout tried to act with moderation and in a conciliatory spirit, but his opponents have nevertheless not been satisfied. Selfishness and unlawful ambition do not find gratification in mere words. Besides, Cashmere officials, with some exceptions, are notorious for their malpractices, and most of them are therefore averse to a well-centralised administration with a wise and united organisation at its head.

Then, the Maharaja is impotent to

appoint his own advisers or to remove them. The consequence is that, in all cases in which their interests clash with his, they feel inclined to prefer the former to the detriment of the latter. Hence arise friction and the absence of that cordiality and co-operation without which it is impossible that the affairs of the State should go on smoothly and prosperously. I humbly submit that to remove this friction and ensure this cordiality and co-operation, it is essential that the Maharaja's advisers should be rendered dependent upon His Highness, so that, owing allegiance to him, they might not feel tempted to disregard his authority, but might identify their interests with and subordinate their wishes to his. However anxious the Maharaja may be to place the administration upon a sound and satisfactory footing, he can never accomplish his object till he secures the services of some thoroughly honest and capable men, who may serve him unselfishly with zeal and energy, and while helping him with wholesome and vigorous counsel, may work in obedience to and conformity with his directions. No position is more invidious and galling than that of a master with intractable servants and subordinates who can walk over his head, and the Maharaja can never hope to gain his object as long as he does not receive the warmest support and is not invested with adequate authority to enforce discipline and maintain order.

Thus expediency and justice both demand that the Maharaja should be rescued from his present predicament, and policy, I submit, also dictates the same course. At this moment, when the Russians are causing consternation from their fastnesses in Central Asia, the goodwill and attachment of our Princes and Chiefs, one of the 'best mainstays,' as Lord Canning called them, for the defence of the Empire, should be thoroughly conciliated; and nothing can so well further the attainment of this object as the rendition of Cashmere to its rightful ruler.

The Dogras, besides, are subjects of the Maharaja to whom they are devotedly attached, and they are among the flower of the Indian Army. A just, fair and considerate treatment of the Maharaja is sure to inspire them with greater ardour and incite them to greater self-sacrifice, bravery and heroism. The Maharaja's loyalty and devotion to the Paramount Power, which have been so conspicuously displayed on previous occasions, would also receive a fresh stimulus, and his noble example would act and react vigorously on his subjects. A strong, well-governed and contented Cashmere would constitute an effective bulwork against external aggressions, maintain peace and order in the border districts, and considerably strengthen the line of frontier defences. The Maharaja, fully conscious of his responsible position in the Empire, would be encouraged to serve with increased earnestness and zeal and neglect no measures calculated to promote and solidify imperial interests. And the Government of India would regain its former place, in respect of its good faith to the people and the Princes, in the minds of the Indian population. An act, fraught with so much good, carries with it its own recommendation, and hardly requires any arguments to press it upon the approval of the wise and the far-seeing.

It may be contended that there is the Resident to help the Maharaja in all his difficulties. This contention looks plausible at first sight, but a little examination will shew that it is not a sound one. Firstly, it is unjust to retain the Maharaja any longer under the Resident's control; secondly, it is proper and reasonable that the Maharaja should be allowed a free hand to set his house in order when he has given abundant evidence that he is competent to do so; and lastly, the help of the Resident cannot be always available to the Maharaja, even if the Resident were at all times ready and willing to afford it to him. The Resident cannot always be on the spot; but even if he were or could be, it would not be consistent with the dignity nor conducive to the interests of the Maharaja to be constantly complaining against his own subordinates. Complaints, moreover, to be effectual, must entail enquiries, and these cannot but contribute to weaken and render unpleasant the Maharaja's position in very many instances. It is easy to conceive that there may be numerous occasions on which the Maharaja may be slighted, conspired against and baffled, without his being able to establish the guilt of the offending parties. The only sure and practical remedy against the Maharaja's difficulties, therefore, consists in strengthening his hands by restoring to him his full powers, and according to him the generous sympathy and support of the Government of India.

I have already alluded to the fact that the Maharaja never enjoyed perfect independence of action, and that much of his failure is to be attributed to this cause. The Maharaja thus expressed himself on the point in his letter to Lord Lansdowne four years and a half ago—'Now, to put it very plainly, I have never up to this time enjoyed complete independence of action in State affairs—some sort of pressure or other has always been put upon me since my accession to the throne, and I have never been free to administer the State according to my internal satisfaction. Under such circumstances, it has been very cruel indeed to hold me *personally* responsible for any maladministration and punish me severely as a criminal.' The Maharaja then added —'If your Excellency really wants to make me responsible for the administration of the State, (and I am very glad and ready to take such responsibility on my head), I would ask to be a responsible ruler. In spite of what has been represented against me about my incapacity &c. &c., I would ask your Excellency to give me a fair trial in order to see what I do for the furtherance [of the wishes] of the Supreme Government and the prosperity of the State. From three to five years' time is quite sufficient for me to put everything into order from the date of holding responsibility; provided I am allowed full strength and independence to choose my own councillors and ministers'.*

It must be admitted that the Maharaja put his case very strongly in a few words, and that his request about choosing his own councillors and ministers must be regarded as a *sine qua non* for his success as a ruler. It is to be sincerely hoped that Lord Lansdowne will, now at least, after the lapse of four years and a half, be pleased to sanction the trial which the Maharaja then so earnestly prayed for. Let Col. Prideaux once more return to Cashmere to help and guide the Maharaja with his sympathetic counsel, let the Maharaja appoint his own councillors and ministers,—men of character, education, tact and ability, who owing their appoint-

*Maharaja's letter to the Viceroy, dated 14 May 1889.

ment to him, may identify their interests with his and heartily co-operate with him in all matters pertaining to the government of the State—and let the Resident's restraining hand be withdrawn and his Highness set free from the strings which now hold him ; and Cashmere shall make rapid strides towards that consummation which the Maharaja has longed for, though in vain, during the last eight years. The Maharaja will be able to vindicate his own reputation as a ruler, Cashmere will rise to the dignity of a 'model' Indian State, the Dogras will fight with still greater enthusiasm the battles of the Indian Empire, the minds of the Princes and Chiefs will be set at rest, the confidence of the people in the good faith of the Paramount Power will be fully re-established, the British Government will find it easier to defy the attempts of Russia in central Asia, and Lord Lansdowne will accomplish a just and graceful act which will earn him a lasting place in the grateful remembrance of the present and ſuture generations of this vast continent.